STOP SMOKING NATURALLY

Stop Smoking
Naturally

MARTHA WORK ASHELMAN

KEATS PUBLISHING

LOS ANGELES

NTC/Contemporary Publishing Group

Library of Congress Cataloging-in-Publication Data

Ashelman, Martha Work.
    Stop smoking naturally / Martha Work Ashelman.
        p. cm.
    Includes bibliographical references and index.
    ISBN 0-658-00384-4 (pbk.)
        1. Cigarette habit—Psychological aspects. 2. Smoking—
Prevention. 3. Nicotine—Physiological effect. 4. Smoking cessation
programs. I. Title.

HV5740 .A75 2000
613.85—dc21   00-041256

Published by Keats Publishing
A division of NTC/Contemporary Publishing Group, Inc.
4255 West Touhy Avenue, Lincolnwood, Illinois 60646-1975 U.S.A.

Managing Director and Publisher: Jack Artenstein
Executive Editor: Peter L. Hoffman
Director of Publishing Services: Rena Copperman
Managing Editor: Jama Carter
Project Editor: Claudia McCowan

Text design: Laurie Young

Printed and bound in the United States of America

International Standard Book Number: 0-658-00384-4
00 01 02 03 04 TK 18 17 16 15 14 13 12 11 10 9 8 7 6 5 4 3 2 1

I dedicate this book to Tom Strange, a gifted addiction therapist, who successfully broke free of smoking in my class in 1987 and became my helper and mentor. Special gratitude also goes to Dr. Terrie Elliott, whose input in stress management has been invaluable. Finally, to my daughter, Ruth Crane, for editing, advising, and caring.

Contents

FOREWORD

My heart was pounding with anxiety as I pulled off the highway at Berkeley Springs, West Virginia. I was on my way to a rustic mountain resort where Martha Ashelman was running one of only a handful of residential smoking cessation programs in the country.

I had read all the material and still wasn't convinced. But I knew I had to do something. I had been smoking for far too long, and my body was telling me, "Enough!"

Like almost everyone who came to Martha's weeklong program, I had already tried everything: the patches, the gum, gritting my teeth, and any number of nicotine substitution gimmicks. The truth was, I was addicted to a drug more potent than heroin.

Martha's approach was a refreshing change from the other programs and lectures I had attended. She was convinced we could "break free from smoking" by pampering ourselves rather than suffering through the extended periods of deprivation I knew all too well.

Now, after running the program for thirteen years, Martha Ashelman has developed this self-help book so that others may benefit from her wisdom. While I found that getting away to a mountain resort for a weeklong program offered a healthy environment to overcome the most difficult and nagging challenge of my life, I believe her program as detailed in this book can work just as well at home. But since we are talking about making a significant life change, making space in your life during that first week can be very useful. Find a local spa and book a massage at least every other day. Also, find a local yoga instructor or aerobics class and attend at least one each day. Sound self-indulgent? It is, and you deserve it!

As detailed in this book, Martha's rules for breaking free are simple:

1. *Drink lots and lots of water.* During the first several months, I drank more than a gallon of water daily. At first the water helped flush nicotine from my system. It then served as an effective substitute for smoking. Every time I thought of smoking, I reached for the bottle and drank as much water as I could stomach. Martha also explains another benefit. By keeping yourself hydrated, your urges to smoke diminish significantly. During the first weeks of breaking free, my strongest urges came when I had not been drinking enough water. Water also helps prevent weight gain.

2. *Breathe deeply.* As a smoker, I discovered I had been depriving myself of one of the most precious physical joys in life—taking in a deep breath. Cigarettes were choking my sense of smell and denying me a wonderful feeling of being able to breathe deeply without coughing. Within a few days, I noticed a remarkable difference. Deep breathing became even more rewarding than a cigarette and my energy and stamina soared.

3. *Exercise.* Martha put us on a simple daily routine that revolved around physical exercise. We began the day with a light thirty-minute walk, followed by a half-hour stretching class. After breakfast, we filled our days with classes in aerobics, dance, yoga, and even T'ai Chi. The exercise kept me busy during those first frightening days, and the exertion served as a minute-by-minute reminder of the new body I had to look forward to. During the first several months of breaking free, every time I faced an urge to smoke, I got up and walked for fifteen minutes. That's about as long as a cigarette break. The difference was, when I returned from the walk, I sat down at my desk more energized and focused and not smelling like a stale ashtray. Drinking so much water also means more trips to the bathroom, which I turn into more opportunities to exercise.

4. *Diet.* What we eat has a direct effect on cravings. Martha will put you on a healthy high-alkaline diet, which had a major impact on my cravings. But when I indulged in fatty foods like beef, my cravings returned with a vengeance. A great tip: as soon as you finish a

meal, get up and walk or do something. The habit of sitting around after eating is asking for trouble. Also, avoid sugar as much as possible.

5. *Pamper yourself.* This is a program of nursing yourself back to health with a lot of TLC and self-nurturing. Until I broke free, I rewarded myself with a cigarette at every turn, but Martha taught me new nurturing ways that were far more enjoyable. I had four massages during my first week, did yoga twice, and went to two T'ai Chi classes. Each experience was my reward to myself for the progress I was making.

During my first week of breaking free from smoking, I actually lost 10 pounds and felt healthier than I had in years. Others in my class did not lose weight, but no one gained any either.

I am not saying that Martha has discovered a magical or even easy way to quit smoking. All that exercise, drinking all that water, and eating all that salad took work and commitment. But I can say that by the end of the third day, I remember feeling so elated because for the first time in years, my mind was not consumed with smoking, and I was no longer organizing my life around my next cigarette. In this book, Martha provides a step-by-step guide so you can reorganize your life around things that make you feel good.

Martha doesn't bother with the scare tactics many smoking cessation programs rely on. She assumes anyone picking up this book already knows cigarettes are hazardous to human health. She assumes we already know smoking is the leading preventable public health epidemic. Instead, Martha helps to demystify smoking, addiction, and the process of breaking free. She makes us conscious of just how long a craving lasts, and how different foods can reduce—or increase—cravings. And she gives us very specific things to do.

Perhaps most important, Martha teaches us that breaking free from smoking requires one significant life change: Whether we want to admit it or not, over the years, a cigarette becomes a smoker's best friend. To successfully break free, we have to commit to ending that friendship and replace it with new friends, beginning with ourselves. Martha emphasizes the need to treat ourselves with compassion and love, which is surely what we would do for any other friend. Imagine treating yourself to a massage every so often. Imagine taking the time at night to draw a nice hot bath before bed. Imagine waking up each morning and giving yourself a big bear hug to congratulate yourself for all you have accomplished.

One final note: Relapse is a genuine concern. Chances are you have been smoking for many years and cigarettes have become an ingrained habit, a way of life. Changing all that takes time. Three months after attending Martha's program, I relapsed, bumming a cigarette from a friend. I got dizzy, just like that first time I picked up a cigarette, and by the end of the day I was addicted again. Within a week, I returned to Martha's West Virginia retreat and for three days immersed myself in exercise, water, and Martha's diet. It worked. By this time I was able to take the program with me everywhere I went. With this book, you can too. Now please excuse me while I go drink another few glasses of water!

—BRIAN BARGER, DIRECTOR, INTERNATIONAL TRAUMA
RESOURCE CENTER, SILVER SPRING, MARYLAND

INTRODUCTION

The Break Free program, which I have developed and taught over the past thirteen years, attempts to help addicted smokers make lifestyle changes that will reinforce their choice to remain free of smoking. This program makes them conscious of all the elements of their smoking behavior and is explained in a usable, self-help manner in this book.

The course is "holistic," in that it points out to the participants a wide range of beliefs and attitudes they have about smoking and health that have hampered their ability to break free of cigarettes and shows them the benefits of breaking free of smoking for the body, mind, and spirit. Smokers don't realize that they have forfeited their ability to make wise choices about their lives and health to the nicotine in their bodies.

Smokers can't break free of cigarettes until they are ready. Most want to be free, but their nicotine-drenched brains can't help them make the decision to be free. Picking up this book is an indication that you might accept help and have enough motivation to start the process. Now you can assess all your valid reasons for wanting to be free of smoking. Revisiting these reasons frequently will keep your motivation active.

Most dedicated smokers do not eat a healthy diet nor do they get enough exercise. Many equate the notion of "healthy food" with sawdust and tofu. By concentrating on tasty foods with a high alkaline content, most people have only moderate withdrawal symptoms. Because fear of gaining weight keeps many people (particularly women) smoking against their will, I also spend at least one session explaining why weight gain does not necessarily need to be the outcome of smoking cessation.

I personally believe that it is impossible to stay free of smoking without a regular exercise program. In fact, I tell the group on the second day after they have become free of smoking that the answer to any question I ask is "exercise." You can explore all the exercise options offered and find some activity that interests you or meets your needs. I particularly recommend walking—even mall walking.

Another important component in the program is paying attention to the concept of a "higher power," which can be understood in either religious or secular terms. Participants are taught several meditation techniques, as well as correct breathing. Several massages are included in my residential program, and I suggest these as a reward for becoming free of smoking.

Stop Smoking Naturally is separated into three sections. The first is concerned with building up the motivation to become free, overcoming obstacles, understanding the nature of addiction to nicotine, preparing carefully for the day you break free, and, finally, making the break.

The second section is full of information that will help you in the process of breaking free: the nature of cravings and urges, understanding possible withdrawal symptoms, an analysis of the benefits of certain foods, and the need to drink copious amounts of water. This section also includes a description of relaxation methods, exercise options, and specific rules for preventing weight gain.

The third section deals with the medical aspects of smoking. One might think that the awful consequences of smoking should be listed in the front of the book, but the truth is that very few smokers are motivated to stop smoking by fear. After you are free of smoking, you are better able to understand its dangers and can rejoice in the major damage control you have accomplished.

The final chapter shows how you can avoid relapse. Throughout the book are warnings that one puff is too many, and that the danger of relapse is close for some time after you are free of smoking. This is a summary of positive actions you can take to remain free.

xxi

Recognizing the
Need to Be Free

The most precious thing you have in life is your health. This is probably the primary reason you picked up this book. You know cigarettes are affecting your health. You have begun to understand how good health or poor health influences your actions, thoughts, and beliefs. And now you have come to realize that cigarettes have been stealing your health and have taken charge of your life.

Why did it take you so long to "get it"? Smoking is not an occasional pastime; it's an addiction to a substance that has taken over your body, mind, and soul. And now it is time to break free!

I have a problem when someone says, "I've got to quit smoking." To me, "quit" has a negative, almost submissive connotation. Compare "quitting" with the positive elation that will envelop you when you have finally broken free of the grip of nicotine. The dictionary meaning of *quit* includes the phrase "to stop trying." Quitting sounds almost passive to me, as if some external force is handling your situation; breaking free, on the other hand, is clearly a dynamic action that shows your commitment to taking charge of your life in a positive rather than negative manner.

FIND THE PASSION

Where does the passion to be free of cigarettes come from? It comes from that inner voice that says, "Who is in charge? What is going on here? I can't even wake up without a cigarette. I can't drive my car without a cigarette. I can't even make love unless I'm sure I've lined up the smokes for after." Now, really, who or what is in charge?

Where is the passion to take charge of your life and the strength to do it? The passion, the commitment, is somewhere inside you, and you can find it. You can reinforce your resolve to be free—a day at a time, using the tools you will find in this book.

How do you feel about coating the inside of your body with a yellowish film that also covers your walls and windows? Ugh! As you follow through on your commitment to break away from smoking, you will be getting rid of the poison that you deliberately put into your body every day.

In his documentary *The Medical Aspects of Tobacco,* Dr. Max Snyder says, "Cigarettes are the only substance sold that, when the user follows the instructions carefully, will result in the consumer becoming toxic, chronically ill, or dead!"

Why haven't you stopped? Because the chemical (nicotine) in charge of your brain has told you it would be too difficult. It won't let you break free until you have made that extra effort to pull yourself through the maze of thoughts and deceptions that have kept you on cigarettes. It takes much more effort to not smoke than to smoke. You can learn how to retrain your brain whenever you get that powerful urge. Remember: The urge goes away whether you smoke or not.

BE COMMITTED, NOT INCARCERATED

Your commitment is required. Think of the wonder of your health when you start out on this path to be free. Do you passionately want to preserve your health—that most vital part of you? Do you recognize your health as the gift you were born with and the life force that you surrendered to cigarettes? This is one gift you can take back. With this commitment to your health, you can passionately learn the skills needed to be free of cigarettes one step at time, as you have learned everything else in your life.

WHY IS THIS A HOLISTIC PROGRAM?

I think the word *holistic* is used too indiscriminately; nevertheless, cigarettes have indeed taken over your *whole* body, so a holistic program is needed to get your whole body back. The program will not always be easy, but when you take charge again, you will find you have the power to make your life rich and full.

I can't emphasize enough that you'll be taking charge of the wonderful human being that you are. Recognize that the life-supporting changes that will come about can truly be a rebirth for you. As we look at nutrition, exercise, and spiritual growth, you will find that you have the tools within yourself to break free. You don't need the patch, you don't need the gum, you don't need the spray, and you probably don't need a mood-elevating drug. We'll deal with that later.

We will go through the whole process one step at a time; I'll offer help and suggestions to change nutrition patterns, particularly if you are concerned about gaining weight. You will find an exercise program to incorporate into your life that is beneficial, enjoyable, and designed to make sure you don't gain weight.

ADMIT YOUR AMBIVALENCE

All smokers who are determined to break free also want the freedom to smoke whenever they want to. Wouldn't that be a perfect world? However, the addiction will always take hold if you try to have it both ways.

There are some alcoholics who can take an occasional drink. Studies done by the National Institute of Drug Abuse have shown that alcoholics are out of control 10 percent of the time, but cigarette smokers (smokaholics) are out of control 90 to 95 percent of the time. Most chronic alcoholics can limit themselves to drinking at certain times or places, such as after sundown or only on weekends, and can manage occasional relapses of binge drinking. Although they are addicted to alcohol, most alcoholics don't become drunk on a daily basis, and they have a certain amount of control over their addiction.

Addicted cigarette smokers, on the other hand, usually consume their maximum number of cigarettes on a daily basis and are not able to stop for even a day or two. Addicted smokers whose smoking is restricted at work or in social situations usually make up for the nicotine deficiency by "loading" or "chain smoking" when they are free to smoke. Being deprived for a few hours causes withdrawal symptoms, which the smoker relieves by smoking. Many people have told me that they smoked even when they were too sick to smoke or had promised themselves they would not smoke another cigarette at a particular time. They were not able to control their consumption until they made the choice to be completely free of cigarettes.

So, your chances of being free of smoking while still having an occasional cigarette are about the same as winning the lottery. I find that participants in my groups are universally nervous and full of anxiety at the thought of becoming free of cigarettes. Without exception, there is a feeling of ambivalence—because nicotine is still in charge of thoughts about being free of it.

THE TRICKS OF THE TRADE

You may be wondering what exactly you will have to do to break free of smoking. Your first task will be to deal with your rationalizations for smoking. If you have said, "But I enjoy it," what you really said was, "I might enjoy one or two a day, but the rest are part of the addiction." You will have to discard some of your illusions.

This book will show you how to manufacture endorphins in positive ways rather than by smoking. (Endorphins, which our brains produce from time to time, create warm feelings of well-being. This crash course in positive thinking will not allow you to wallow in your gloom. You won't be able to stay in the mood that makes you think you need a cigarette or that without one, you've lost your "best friend."

You must be alert every second. Let's say you are walking in the country, and you decide to cross the road. You look right, then left. You start to cross the road, but you hear a car coming. You take another look to the right, and sure enough—a car is coming from that direction. That's paying attention. Bring your smoking patterns into your consciousness and take a good look in all directions.

6

HOW YOUR SMOKING AFFECTS THOSE WHO CARE ABOUT YOU

In one of my programs, a woman expressed that she did not want her mother, who had pressured her for years to give up cigarettes, to know she had stopped smoking. The group suggested that she let her mother know that she had achieved freedom from cigarettes in spite of the pressure, not because of it.

Those who care for you, such as your spouse, parents, children, or friends, have probably told you often that smoking is harmful and that you should stop. This was of course not news to you, but the ways in which the message was conveyed might have influenced you to put off stopping. The decision to be free of smoking is yours alone, and you alone will achieve success. You might need to make this distinction clear to someone who has been nagging you about cigarettes and might want to take some responsibility for your glory. Remember, it's easy to be right about the dangers of cigarettes. All those people out there who don't smoke are right!

Nonsmokers have better health, they have more stamina, and they're not aging too fast. However, we who have smoked do have one thing up on them: We will achieve this goal of breaking free and it will be one of the greatest accomplishments of our lives.

7

When people put themselves through the stress of breaking free of cigarettes for anyone but themselves, they are doomed to failure. It is important that they examine the people in their lives who are putting pressure on them to stop smoking. There is something about human nature that makes it difficult to let those who have been the cheering or jeering section be right. So if your mother, spouse, or children have been pressuring you heavily to get off cigarettes, and you are taking the leap to please them —forget it. Work on making this your choice, and your choice alone. You need to be totally clear about this, because choosing to be free from smoking is a long-term commitment.

Acceleration with Motivation: Climb Aboard the Freedom Express!

Don't look back. You made the choice to be free of cigarettes and you are on your way. The journey may take a while, but you are about to learn the skills that will keep you motivated. You can now make a careful assessment of the many benefits of breaking free of smoking versus the grip nicotine has had on your soul.

CHOICE, NOT DEPRIVATION

Have you ever considered why it has been so difficult for you to stop smoking? Regardless of method—gum, the patch, acupuncture—you experienced the feeling of deprivation and the urge to smoke overtook you. You could not wallow for long in the despair of deprivation before you finally succumbed and went back to smoking. From the moment you deprived yourself of cigarettes, you were setting yourself up to smoke again, rather than choosing to be free.

You have probably heard stories or seen movies in which long-term prisoners of war, upon their release, are handed a cigarette by some kind soul. If they were smokers before being captured, they truly suffered from deprivation during their captivity. Their first puff on that cigarette is nostalgic and comforting, and though they may get sick from the toxicity, they fall right back into the trap of smoking, believing that cigarettes are a reward.

Thoughts of deprivation feed your need for a cigarette. Choosing to be free of cigarettes offers you positive options as you reflect on the many benefits of being free. What you say to yourself is very important in maintaining your motivation in the initial stages of freedom. I will offer you positive affirmations, and you will undoubtedly find your own mental message to keep you in the winning mode. Dwelling on feeling deprived has kept many people from going beyond the first step toward freedom from cigarettes.

Believe that deprivation is a positive choice. By choosing to give up cigarettes, you actually escaped unjustified imprisonment in "Marlboro Country," where you were deprived of all the benefits of being free of nicotine; rather, you declared your independence from smoking. You chose the benefits of breaking free.

DEFINING YOUR MOTIVATION

Even though you may still be ambivalent about your choice to be free of cigarettes, you have already toyed with the idea that "now is the time to stop." How many times have you said to yourself, "I'll finish this pack tonight and then I'll stop tomorrow"? Were you telling yourself that "now" had come—that you were finally "ready"? Probably not. Still in denial, you were hoping the fairy princess would come in the night, tap your forehead with her magic wand, and say, "Now you are free of cigarettes—but you can smoke when you want to." So far you have not been on her scheduled rounds. Her real message is, "It's up to you."

Motivate yourself with the thought, "Now I will take the first steps to being free." Take the word *try* out of your vocabulary and proceed with the belief that you have made the commitment and are ready to learn to use the tools you need to leave cigarettes behind forever.

THE BENEFITS OF
BREAKING FREE OF SMOKING

Now is the time to weigh the benefits of breaking free of smoking with the so-called pleasure you got from your addiction. When you recognize the fantastic benefits of regaining control of your life versus the powerlessness of being a smoker, the choice should be very clear.

Think of how much better your life will be without cigarettes. Every smoker's situation is different, so you must make the
choices and value the benefits enough to work through the pain
of going without cigarettes. Your reasons for choosing to break
free are the important thoughts your mind will return to over and
over again in the next few days and months. But, as Denis Waitley
writes in *The Psychology of Winning,* "Our mind goes to our fears
as if they were our goals." Keep your motivation full of winning
thoughts, and your mind will make you free of smoking.

Physical Benefits of Being Free of Smoking

Don't refer to chapter 13, which lists in great detail the medical
hazards of smoking, until you are free of cigarettes. You would
probably diagnose yourself as having every bad symptom.
However, keeping in mind your intense motivation to be free
now, choose from the following list the physical benefits you
would like to start enjoying immediately once you stop smoking.
Number your choices by priority.

____ Hands and feet become warmer from improved
circulation.

____ Blood pressure and pulse rate lower and approach
normal.

____ Mouth and hair no longer smell of smoke.

____ Senses of taste and smell improve.

____ Cough disappears and phlegm production returns
to normal.

____ Stamina increases significantly.

12

_____ Energy level is higher.

_____ Field of vision increases by 15 to 20 percent.

_____ Risk of all diseases caused by smoking is reduced—emphysema, heart attacks, and cancers of all types.

_____ Other physical benefits _____

Emotional Benefits of Being Free of Smoking

You can now begin to sort out your emotional attachment to your "best friend"—the one who is betraying you. Your nicotine-drenched brain has made it difficult for you to evaluate your feelings about cigarettes. You were forced to say you enjoyed them, because in all other matters you are a rational being. And why would a rational being who recognizes that smoking is unpleasant, irritating, and harmful do it anyway? Many people admit that they often smoke against their own will. Now number in order of priority the emotional benefits you will get minutes after you break free!

_____ You have improved your self-image.

_____ You have put yourself in charge of your life.

_____ You have a feeling of accomplishment and self-respect.

_____ You are becoming happier, less depressed.

_____ Never again will you have to plan every activity around cigarette smoking.

_____ Never again will you have to make excuses, or feel guilty about needing cigarettes.

_____ Never again will you have to go back into the house to be sure all cigarettes are extinguished.

13

_____ ver again will you have to take inventory of
_____ oking paraphernalia before you leave your home
_____ office.

_____ Now you can hold on to the excitement of being a winner and bask in a sense of well-being.

Personal Social Benefits

In addition to the physical and emotional benefits, think of the social benefits that take place immediately after you break free of smoking. Number in order of priority some of the social benefits that you will enjoy.

14

_____ You now project an image of self-control that is not available to smokers.

_____ Your house, car, and clothes don't smell of cigarettes.

_____ You will have more time to devote to family and friends.

_____ You will not become a burden on your family members because of illnesses related to smoking cigarettes.

_____ You can pay normal insurance rates.

_____ You can patiently enjoy social situations that last more than an hour.

Financial Benefits of Being Free of Smoking

There must have been a time when you said that if cigarettes reached a certain price, you would give them up. Unfortunately that time came and went, and you are spending a good deal more in today's dollars for cigarettes than you did when you started. You can figure it out using the chart on page 16.

Think of the wonderful rewards you can give yourself with all the money you will be putting in the cookie jar every day.

SEEKING SELF-ESTEEM

The question of breaking free of cigarettes, after you have weighed all the benefits against the addictive pleasure, may center on "Am I up to it?" The answer has a great deal to do with your opinion of yourself.

The term *self-esteem* wasn't part of mainstream American culture until the 1960s. The Puritan ethic governed much of child-rearing practices, and it was not thought proper to be too proud or boastful. Those of you who came into adulthood believing in your self-worth won't have to do the exercises I am including to help you feel worthy of a long and productive life. However, if you know that smoking is an evil force that is destroying the essence of your life, and you are beating yourself up about not stopping, you probably need to work on self-esteem.

I believe you can build up your self-esteem by taking measure of your accomplishments and the goodness and common sense that is within you. Answer the following questions and see if you can enhance your self-esteem.

1. What comes to mind as the best thing you have ever accomplished?
2. Do you think that being free of smoking will equal that? Exceed that?

15

3. Who are you stopping smoking cigarettes for?

4. Knowing that you are a kind, intelligent, thoughtful person who has a high level of self-esteem, what could possibly break your resolve to be free of cigarettes?

5. What are you most proud of?

6. Will being free of smoking give you a better feeling of self-worth?

7. Did you ever get an award? Did you deserve it?

8. Are you worthy of a long and productive life free of the tyranny of smoking?

9. Who are the people in your life whom you love, and who love you?

10. Do you believe you can and will stay free of smoking?

16

Cost of Smoking Cigarettes Per Year

1. Estimate number of packs smoked per day (use decimals) _____

   (Example: 1¾ packs per day = 1.75)

2. Multiply line #1 by 365 for number of packs per year _____

3. Multiply line #2 by cost per pack for cost per year _____

4. TOTAL COST OF CIGARETTES PER YEAR $_____

Indirect Cost from My Smoking Habit Per Year

Lighters and other paraphernalia _____

Lost work due to smoking-related illness _____

Additional dental/medical care and prescriptions _____

Higher health insurance premiums
(about 5 percent) _____

Extra trips to store to buy cigarettes _____

Burned clothing, furniture, and carpets _____

Extra cleaning of house, drapes, and
car to remove odor _____

Extra dry cleaning of clothing to
remove odor _____

Other related expenses _____

    5. TOTAL INDIRECT COST PER YEAR $_____

Yearly Cost of Smoking Habit

    6. Add lines #4 and #5 $_____

Cost of Smoking Habit to Date

    7. Multiply line #6 by the number
       of years I have smoked $_____

Cost of Continuing to Smoke

    8. Subtract present age from 69
       (average smoker's life expectancy)
       for number of years I could
       still waste money _____

    9. Multiply line #8 by line #6 for

FUTURE SAVINGS FROM BREAKING FREE NOW $_____

    10. Subtract my present age from
        76 (the average nonsmoker's
        life expectancy) for number of
        years I can save money _____

    11. Multiply line #10 by line #6 for

FUTURE LIFETIME SAVINGS $_____

THE SERENITY PRAYER

Over the years, many participants in my program have taught me a great deal about overcoming addiction. I am particularly grateful for the positive contributions from people who have been through twelve-step programs. The *Serenity Prayer* can be a reality check throughout your day:

> God grant me the serenity to accept the things
> I cannot change,
> The courage to change the things I can,
> And the wisdom to know the difference.

You know you have the courage to start on this journey to freedom and that you have escaped your rationalization that it is "impossible" to be free of cigarettes. Keep this prayer in your satchel of good motivators.

Overcoming
Obstacles to Freedom

THE FEAR OF SUCCESS

It is important to remember that in any attempt to break free of smoking you either fail or succeed. Success permanently frees you from the tyranny of tobacco, and you will soon become aware that in becoming free of cigarettes you are creating a new identity. Chances are that you started smoking before you were eighteen years old; if so, you have never experienced adult life without cigarettes. Recognize that success will give you a different perspective on yourself and that freedom from the bondage of tobacco will alter your entire life.

Don't pay much attention to failure. It should be very familiar to you, because every day you follow the same old mode that keeps you in bondage to cigarettes. Even if you should return to smoking after a short period, some lessons of hope can be learned. It is important to remember that failure may increase your chance of success on your next serious attempt.

PREDICTORS OF SUCCESS

Previous Attempts

Several factors help predict your success in breaking free of smoking. The first is previous attempts to quit, which demonstrated your awareness of the need to be free of cigarettes and your determination to keep on trying. These attempts were not failures but rehearsal periods—however brief—in which you adjusted to life without cigarettes and almost conquered "Old Nick." With these attempts to break free behind you, you can more easily convince yourself that the next one will result in freedom.

Willingness to Make Sacrifices

You must be willing to make some sort of monetary sacrifice to demonstrate your commitment. This might include buying tapes or a book, paying for a structured program, or making an appointment with your doctor to get a prescription for some medication that might help. You might want to make a small wager with a friend that you will stay free for a certain length of time, and raise the ante for up to a year. In May of 1999, Dr. Julian Whitaker, whose holistic-health newsletter is full of wisdom, declared that he was too fat and was going to lose 20 pounds in three months. If he did not reach this goal, he pledged to give $10,000 to

President Clinton's legal defense fund. Such a gift would have been against his convictions, so he was motivated to reach his weight-loss goal easily.

Putting money and time on the line shows that you are committed to change and ready to follow through on being free of cigarettes.

Multifaceted Solutions

Another predictor of success is having multifaceted solutions for:

- Dealing with possible weight gain
- Managing irritability and anger
- Developing an exercise plan

21

Some of the solutions might be nutritional counseling, relaxation and meditation skills, and other behavior modification techniques.

Support Groups

A factor of success that is particularly important to women is joining a long-term support group. See chapter 5 for support group suggestions. Many individuals who have gone through my residential program have become support group leaders. Helping someone else become free of cigarettes is the best kind of reinforcement you can get.

In this book we will touch on a number of proven techniques to help you through the initial stages of cessation. When you have committed to developing skills to cope with the inevitable changes that will come about in your life, you are well on your way to freedom from smoking.

Addictive Behavior

Terry smoked her first cigarette soon after her morning alarm sounded and her last right before she went to sleep at night. She couldn't make a phone call without first checking her cigarette supply. She once lost her ski pole when it fell from the chairlift while she searched for matches in her parka. She couldn't go through a meal without a cigarette. In the middle of the night she would smoke a cigarette. She'd search though ashtrays looking for long butts to smoke again. And if she ran out of cigarettes late at night, she would get dressed and drive to the nearest convenience store. Terry tried several times to stop smoking, but it wasn't until she came to understand that cigarettes would ruin her health that she finally stopped for good.

Bill Mayhugh, who was a radio drive-time host in the Washington, D.C., area for many years, eagerly shares his story and method of stopping smoking. In fact, he has put on tape the revelation that enabled him to break free. Mayhugh thinks that the difference between *knowing* and *believing* that smoking destroys your health is the difference between failure and success in breaking free. "To *know* is to have knowledge of something," Bill says. "To *believe* is to accept as fact that which you know." There isn't a smoker out there who doesn't know that smoking is harmful to his or her health.

Bill knew that his "friend" was killing him, but he had a deep fear of going through the trauma of deprivation. Knowing smoking will harm you and shorten your life won't necessarily make you overcome your addiction and give up cigarettes. Truly believing that smoking has been causing major health damage and is shortening your life by many years will certainly make you take notice and do something about it.

An analogy may bring this home to you. Many of us grew up with asbestos in our homes and had no knowledge that it might harm us and shorten our lives. But after the overwhelming evidence became public about the dangers of asbestos to those who had to work with it or live in an environment saturated by it, everyone knew that asbestos was harmful, and they believed it as well. The aerobics studio in the spa where I have taught for many years has a ceiling sprayed with a bumpy white substance that is made of cellulose. I often ask a class, "What do you think the ceiling is made of?" When nobody answers, I say, "asbestos." Then I hear sounds of horror and disbelief. Everyone knows and believes asbestos is harmful, and they are incredulous that the spa would expose them to that danger—until they realize that I was jesting.

You know smoking is harmful, but you keep on doing it. When you arrive at the point that you believe that cigarettes will do irreversible harm to your body, you will then act on that belief and break free of smoking.

To get you from the stage of knowing to believing, you need to learn all you can about how cigarettes affect your body. In recent years the evidence has become overwhelming that cigarettes are bad, bad things. They increase the smoker's risk of death and illness from a wide variety of diseases. The National Institute on Drug Abuse has estimated that, in the United States

23

alone, smoking is responsible for at least 350,000 premature deaths a year. Other estimates are as high as 540,000.

SMOKING ROULETTE

How did you convince yourself that you will be the lucky one who is spared the consequences of this terrible scourge? When will you pay attention to the nagging physical symptoms that are telling you to believe in your ability to break free from smoking and not succumb to the fear of withdrawal? Your chances of avoiding health problems while you continue to smoke are about the same as your chances of never having an anxious day. Nicotine doesn't miss one cell in your body, so how can you possibly think that it won't cause irreversible damage sometime, some place?

A tragic example of this kind of denial was reported on a June 1999 episode of *60 Minutes*. The United Nations Educational, Scientific and Cultural Organization (UNESCO) had funded a major project in Bangladesh in the 1980s to dig wells in each village so that people would not have to rely on dirty streams and ponds for water. It turned out that 90 percent of the new wells had a high arsenic content, so every time a villager took a drink of water a small amount of bodily damage was done. Eventually everyone was affected, and many thousands have died. When the authorities painted the hazardous wells red and told the villagers that the water was to be used only on gardens or for washing, the villagers denied that the water would harm them because it looked so much cleaner than the rivers and ponds they had been drawing from. This tragedy required a formal apology from the director of UNESCO, a massive effort to educate the people about the realities of their situation, and the creation of a timetable for the restoration of a decent water supply.

You have been in a state of denial similar to the people of Bangladesh because of the overwhelming influence of cigarette advertising campaigns. You may think you were unaffected by the advertisements you read and heard as you were starting out on your cigarette career, but let's see if you can finish the following sentences:

- LSMFT: _____.
- I'd rather fight than _____.
- I'd walk a mile for a _____.
- Joe Camel—eighty-seven years old and still going _____.
- You've come a long way, _____.

When you *know* enough about the hazards of nicotine, you will become aware that every cigarette you smoke harms your body. Read the evidence over and over until you begin to *believe*. The day you truly believe that smoking is ruining your health and your life is the day you will begin to work toward freedom. It can be done. Millions of us have done it, and you can lean on and anticipate support from each and every person who has been successful. I don't believe there is a single person who has successfully broken free of cigarettes who won't rejoice with you in your new freedom and be happy to tell you his story.

The Nature of
Nicotine Addiction

CONSCIOUSLY, PASSIONATELY
TAKE CHARGE OF YOUR LIFE

Cigarettes have been in charge of your life for years. The addiction has been the driving force in all of your conscious actions. Long ago, you had a vague notion that you might get "hooked" on cigarettes, but you had no idea that they would take over your entire existence. You are now in the process of taking back the power and force in your life.

There is no question that cigarettes give you some satisfaction—some of the time. However, after analyzing your smoking as suggested in chapter 2, can you honestly say, "I really enjoy smoking!"? Let's look at what cigarettes have delivered. Then you can work on alternative ways to meet those needs.

What Cigarettes Occasionally Did

- Delivered endorphins—the warm fuzzies that come over you in times of contentment
- Gave you a lift when you were tired
- Helped you to cover up feelings of self-consciousness by having something to fiddle with
- Gave you the opportunity to stall or procrastinate
- Made you think you weren't hungry
- Helped to pass the time when you had to wait

You can probably come up with a few other needs you thought cigarettes met. The only real thing a cigarette ever did for you, however, was take care of your addictive need for another cigarette. Look over the short list above and make realistic suggestions to yourself of how you could meet these needs without smoking.

THE PHYSIOLOGY OF ADDICTION

Although you may have received some good feelings from smoking, you lost the ability to enjoy the massive numbers of cigarettes you smoked, because the addiction took away the pleasure. The 1988 *Surgeon General's Report on Smoking: Nicotine Addiction* verified that nicotine is the addictive compound in tobacco and that tobacco addiction can and should be treated. The report goes on to say that "nicotine is six to eight times more addictive than alcohol."

THE CRITERIA FOR ADDICTION

1. The drug controls the user's behavior. There is a compulsive use of it despite damage to the individual or society, and the drug often becomes a priority—above family, friends, and work.
2. The drug is reinforcing—it is sufficiently rewarding to maintain usage.
3. Tolerance to the drug increases; thus, the individual increases use to recreate the original good feeling.
4. Physical dependence leads to withdrawal symptoms when cigarettes are unavailable, or particularly when an individual tries to stop smoking without a plan.

BREAKING THE ADDICTION
WITH ENERGY AND CONCENTRATION

Be aware that it will take more effort not to smoke than it did to smoke. It will also take energy and concentration. When you understand the steps you must take, the goal is easily reachable. It is important during this process to exercise, watch what you eat, and be careful how you talk to yourself.

THE ADDICTIVE NATURE OF NICOTINE

The effects of nicotine on the brain are staggering.

*   Nicotine affects many systems in the body. It is an addictive drug because it binds to and stimulates the cells of the brain—and it acts fast!

- Nicotine mimics the action of a brain chemical called acetylcholine, binding avidly to nerve cells at specific receptors. This may cause arousal and increased alertness or make you feel relaxed, depending on the time of day and the amount or method of puffing.
- Nicotine is a psychoactive drug that has the power to both relax and stimulate the nervous system. This dual feature of tobacco—it's an upper and a downer—makes it extremely difficult to deactivate the addiction. Nicotine rules—not your brain.
- Nicotine causes neurotransmitters to be released, including those that give a feeling of reward or pleasure as well as those that block pain. These feelings prompt the smoker to repeat its use.
- Nicotine makes you compulsive. In spite of the damage inflicted by tobacco on your health, and its negative social consequences, you continue to use it.
- Your body develops tolerance to nicotine. More and more of the drug is required to produce the original desired effect.
- Withdrawal pain occurs for a few days after breaking free of tobacco.
- Relapse is dangerously close for any smoker who smokes even one cigarette.

SMOKERS' MISGUIDED PERCEPTIONS

In his March 1995 *Reader's Digest* article "How Cigarettes Cloud Your Brain," Lowell Ponte explains that almost everyone, including smokers, acknowledges the long-term health risks of smoking. However, most smokers perceive the immediate effect of smoking as something positive—a stimulant that makes them feel more alert, clearheaded, and able to focus on work.

Does smoking actually have these effects? No! The smoker's perception is an illusion. Let's look at what is actually going on in the brain.

Within ten seconds of inhalation, nicotine passes into the bloodstream, transits the barrier that protects the brain from most impurities, and begins to act on the brain cells. As nicotine fits the "keyholes" of acetylcholine, the 1.5 milligrams of nicotine obtained from a cigarette excites the body chemicals, including adrenaline (epinephrine, the principal blood pressure–raising hormone and a heart stimulant and vasoconstrictor) and noradrenaline (norepinephrine, the chemical that transmits epinephrine across synapses in some parts of the central nervous system). This gives you a rush of stimulation and increases the flow of blood to your brain.

If you were wired up to an electroencephalogram (EEG), you would almost immediately record a change in brain-wave patterns. Your brain's output of alpha waves—electrical impulses associated with alert relaxation—dips at first but is restored by the time you finish your first cigarette. The sleep-related delta and theta waves involved in emotions, creative imagery, and deep thought grow weaker.

ALTERED STATE OF MIND

When the cigarette has burned down to nothing, you feel energized and clearheaded. Are you more focused now than a nonsmoking friend or coworker? You may think so, but your improved state of mind is partly due to the fact that you've just ended a period of nicotine deprivation (withdrawal). It won't be long until the next one.

Within thirty minutes, the nicotine you took in is sharply reduced and you feel your energy begin to slip away. You light a second cigarette, and again you feel an adrenaline surge, but the experience is subtly different. Nicotine triggers a cascade of biochemical changes in your brain. A stress-regulating substance called cortisol is released, along with beta-endorphin, the brain's opiatelike pain reliever. With this second cigarette comes one of the paradoxes of smoking: nicotine can either stimulate or soothe, depending on your mood or how you smoke. You feel muscles throughout your body begin to relax, and your pain threshold rises.

Thirty more minutes pass, and your attention drifts away from work and toward the nearby pack of cigarettes. The craving you feel for nicotine is more than psychological, more than a habit or a desire like the one people feel for chocolate or sweets.

Nicotine prompts brain cells to grow many more nicotine receptors than they otherwise would. The brain functions normally despite the unnatural amount of an acetylcholine-like chemical acting on it. Sneaky old nicotine thus reshapes the brain so that a smoker feels normal when nicotine floods her neurons and abnormal when it doesn't.

Smokers live on the edge of a cliff. They are never more than a few hours away from major nicotine withdrawal. A high-level government employee who went through the six days of my smoking cessation program said that he suffered greater withdrawal symptoms sitting though "interminable" policy meetings than he ever did when he set in motion his plan to be free.

32

NICOTINE-INDUCED
ORGANIC MENTAL DISORDER

The American Psychiatric Association classifies smoking withdrawal as a "nicotine-induced organic mental disorder" the symptoms of which include anxiety, irritability, restlessness, insomnia, decreased heart rate, and increased appetite.

In 1978, the Federal Aviation Administration set its present policy of letting airline pilots smoke during flights. The policy remained in place even after smoking by passengers was forbidden. The FAA maintains this policy not because smoking makes pilots more alert but because denying cigarettes to chronic smokers might plunge them into mental impairment while flying.

A 1995 National Institute of Drug Abuse study compared the ability of active smokers to perform simple skill tests with that of "deprived" smokers—those suffering nicotine withdrawal. Smokers who had a cigarette twenty minutes to a half hour before the test initially performed much better on motor tasks than smokers suffering withdrawal. The performance of the active smokers, however, dropped off quickly and soon equaled that of the deprived smokers. The study concluded that nicotine withdrawal causes dramatic mental dysfunction and that all smokers, unless they chain-smoke, suffer the symptoms of withdrawal on a regular, cyclical basis every day.

Let's say that you have already smoked two cigarettes this morning. It is now midmorning when you light your third cigarette. Compared with the first, it tastes flat, but in your true nicotine-addicted fashion, you will soon be lighting the next and the next, almost by reflex. Smokers average thirty cigarettes a day,

33

meaning nearly 110,000 inhalations of nicotine a year. Think of how often that two-fingered gesture of bringing the cigarette to your mouth is repeated—what a habit to break!

Besides the nicotine, those puffs contain carbon monoxide. This gas robs the smoker of oxygen by bonding—at least 200 times more tightly than oxygen—to the hemoglobin that ordinarily delivers oxygen to cells throughout the body. Because of the high level of carbon monoxide, cells cannot pry oxygen atoms loose. It's been said that if a smoker smoked continuously for forty-eight hours at his usual rate of inhalation, he would surely die of carbon monoxide poisoning. This would be due to the significant percentage of hemoglobin made useless by smoking.

How to Rehabilitate
the Pathways in Your Brain

Now that we understand that the brain has developed hundreds of connectors waiting for nicotine to take the place of acetylcholine, we can begin to reprogram the brain's computer. Some of the culprits in the Iran-Contra investigation were surprised to find that even though they thought they had deleted all the incriminating evidence from the record, some of it still lurked there. This analogy holds dangerously true for nicotine addiction—you must be alert to the supposedly "deleted" addiction waiting to take you hostage again and keep you from freedom. In chapter 14, we will pay special attention to reprogramming the brain to prevent relapse.

CAVEAT TO CONSULTING
YOUR PHYSICIAN FOR ADVICE

Researchers surveyed nearly every accredited medical school in the country and found very little coursework devoted to nicotine dependence, the country's most deadly preventable health care problem. A report in the September 1999 issue of the *Journal of the American Medical Association (JAMA)* indicated that U.S. medical school graduates are woefully unprepared to help patients quit smoking. In the 1996 to 1997 school year, 32 out of 102 medical schools dedicated an average of less than one hour of classroom time a year to smoking cessation techniques.

The *JAMA* study found that there was more tobacco-related instruction in the first two years of medical school; only three schools reported having a required course devoted to tobacco education in the third and fourth years. Almost 70 percent of the schools did not require any smoking cessation training at all in the last two years, when students theoretically are learning how to apply their knowledge to patients.

The authors of the study recommend that a model tobacco curriculum be developed and put in place in all U.S. medical schools and that the licensing exam for doctors should pay great attention to the subject. The medical profession usually considers addiction to tobacco less serious than to hard drugs or alcohol. However, I've been told many times by people who have conquered alcohol or hard drugs that nicotine addiction is even more difficult to break away from than heroin.

35

5

Establishing Tapering-Off Strategies

CHOOSING YOUR REASONS TO BREAK FREE OF SMOKING

Take the time to list below at least four reasons for choosing to be free from smoking. Reflect on the many benefits listed in chapter 2. Be specific; for instance:

> I want to be healthy (alive!) to enjoy my grandchildren.
> I want to stop worrying about making a doctor's appointment.
> I want to smell better.

_____

_____

_____

_____

_____

_____

_____

_____

_____

_____

You will be referring to this list often in the next few days and months to keep you focused and motivated.

38

.ℒ♥

CHOOSING THE TIME AND PLACE
TO BREAK FREE

1. Choose the date to be free! Get out your calendar, figure out the best date, and be sure that you are committed to that date and that it is indelible in your mind. I suggest you choose a Friday (if you can take the day off work) or a Saturday, so you will have a couple of days without a set schedule before going back into a normal routine. (I was at home with three young boys when I finally broke free, and there was never a "normal routine.")

2. Choose a pal to be in touch with often during your first day, and frequently during the next couple of weeks. Ideally, this would be someone who is also

becoming free of cigarettes, but it can be a person who has already stopped smoking, or even someone who is still smoking but has expressed a desire to be free of cigarettes and is struggling with setting the time to break free. He is apt to be very sympathetic and would be especially careful to encourage you to stay the course. If you choose someone who is still smoking, you should contact him only by phone on your first day.

You should be willing to share your thoughts and feelings with your pal during the time period you establish together. It must be someone you trust and who doesn't "press your buttons." Choosing such a person may be a good learning tool you will add to your repertoire.

3. You have already set the date and are looking forward to it, preparing yourself and those who love you for this major step in your life. Now understand that you are making the most important choice of your adult life. Begin intense preparation at least a week ahead. Since you have accepted the need for change, you can now go about it in a systematic, workable manner until the break-free day.

TAPERING-OFF STRATEGIES

Following are a few of the tapering-off strategies you can choose from to prepare for breaking free. If you choose all of them, you probably will be too busy to smoke at all. Enjoy the challenge.

39

1. Don't smoke until you are completely dressed in the morning.

2. Go to bed at least half an hour after you have smoked the last cigarette of the day.

3. You can smoke half an hour before and half an hour after your first cup of coffee or tea in the morning and any subsequent cups you might have during the day. This exercise will be educational in measuring how closely connected these two habits (addictions) are.

4. You can smoke half an hour before and half an hour after a beverage such as a cocktail or glass of lemonade.

5. Designate locations that are off-limits. See if you can start your car without lighting a cigarette. If you can, don't smoke in it anymore. Choose locations in your home and workplace where you cannot smoke. Remember, you have already made the choice to be free of cigarettes; you are now simply becoming more aware of when and where you smoke.

6. Keep a diary of your feelings and reactions to each cigarette you smoke. This exercise has been a powerful tool in almost every smoking cessation program that has been developed. If you are completely honest, you will learn a great deal about your smoking behavior. This will be helpful when you notice the symptoms of withdrawal after you break free.

7. Buy the least desirable cigarette you can find. You already know which brand that is. Is it a menthol cigarette, or one of the generic brands from a convenience store? This is to remind you that

40

although smoking may have been enjoyable to you at one time, it will now become an increasingly unpleasant experience.

8. Keep cigarettes in an inconvenient place—the trunk of a car, a locked drawer, or a neighbor's house.

9. Smoke with the opposite hand, or wear gloves when you smoke.

10. Don't empty ashtrays until the end of the day.

11. Smoke less of each cigarette.

12. Keep a list with you at all times of your private reasons for wanting to be free from smoking. Write them out on a card that will fit in your wallet. Refer to them often—before each cigarette, if possible.

13. Imagine being a nonsmoker.

14. Talk with friends—both smokers and nonsmokers— about your concerns regarding breaking free.

15. Carefully observe nonsmokers. What do they do after meals? Can they sit quietly and talk? What do they do while they are waiting? This is a very important exercise. You can even tell them why you are observing them. That is certainly an original icebreaker.

16. Sit in nonsmoking areas in places where you have smoked before.

17. Read cigarette ads and study how they are trying to manipulate you to continue smoking. (Who's in charge?)

18. Calculate the money you have spent on cigarettes up to now and what you might have spent in the future. (Refer to the exercise in chapter 2.) Don't forget to

include money spent on medical illnesses that you suspect were smoking related.

19. Make a list of rewards you will enjoy from the money saved by not smoking.

20. Rearrange your environment, particularly the places where you used to smoke. If you were accustomed to smoking while watching TV, move your easy chair to the other side of the room. Do whatever it takes to change things to reflect your new life.

21. Spend time visualizing yourself free of smoking. Close your eyes and mentally go through your usual day, but without cigarettes. Visualize what it's like to get out of bed, get a cup of coffee, read the paper, drive to work, chat with coworkers with whom you used to smoke, sit through a boring meeting, go out to lunch, linger at the table, go through the low-energy time in the afternoon, talk on the phone to a difficult person, drive home, take a walk, enjoy a relaxing time before dinner with your companion, and sit around after dinner watching TV. This may not be your scenario, so write and visualize your own smoke-free day.

SETTING YOUR CLOCK
FOR THE BREAK-FREE DAY

By taking the above actions, you weaken the hold nicotine has over your life. You will probably cut back a great deal on smoking, because you're no longer lighting up mindlessly. Some individuals, however, will smoke more because they are increasingly nervous about the time when they will follow through on their resolve to be free.

If you feel you are not prepared enough by the day you chose to be free, continue to follow the suggestions above. Set a new date to keep your motivation high, and make it soon. During this preparation period, you are getting your mind and body in motion to handle a major change in your lifestyle.

GO SHOPPING

Prepare a shopping list of items you should have on hand for the big day. I have found that the items below are useful for many people.

- Buy crayons and a coloring book, or a crossword or other puzzle book to keep your hands occupied and distract your mind.
- Keep handy several packs of sugarless gum, Popsicle sticks to flick against your teeth, and cinnamon sticks and licorice root to chew on (available at health food stores).
- Wear a wide rubber band, or a fancy ponytail holder, around your wrist and snap it when you need negative reinforcement.
- Buy a couple of new toothbrushes. (As a reward for breaking free, you should get a Sonicare electric toothbrush. They are somewhat expensive but highly recommended by dentists.)

43

- Borrow tapes and books on meditation or motivation from the library. Keep them handy for reference when you have a hard time keeping your thoughts on the positive side. Choose Denis Waitley's *The Psychology of Winning* and *The Power of Resilience,* Thomas Moore's *The Art of Simplicity,* Richard Carlson's *Don't Sweat the Small Stuff,* or almost anything from the Nightingale-Conant series. Play the tapes in your car and listen carefully for a positive message that speaks to you.
- Stock up on healthful snacks at the grocery store: baby carrots, precut celery sticks, all kinds of fresh fruit, and fruit juices. If you have a juicer, plan to use it a great deal in the days to come. If you don't, seriously consider purchasing one. You can use your creativity to make wonderful fruit concoctions that will help kill the urge to smoke and keep your weight down.
- Buy dumbbells, starting at 3 or 5 pounds. These will help you build muscle as part of your new exercise plan. This will be another step in preventing weight gain.

FEAR OF WEIGHT GAIN

Now is the time to examine your feelings about possible—or probable—weight gain. Most people, particularly women, are deeply concerned about gaining weight when they become free. They all have heard horror stories about the correlation between losing cigarettes and gaining pounds. Recognize ahead of time that this may be a problem for you and strategize what you will do about it. This will tend to defuse the issue and help prevent relapse in the months ahead. We will look into this sensitive subject in detail in chapter 12.

EXERCISE IS ALWAYS THE ANSWER

As you go through the process of withdrawal over the first few days, we will deal extensively with the need to put an exercise component into your life. When you exercise regularly after breaking free of cigarettes, you will be better able to cope with the many stresses that may come up.

I recently went through some major stress in my own life and found that walking three to four miles a day was the most wonderful sedative. When the body is in motion, the brain is better able to sort out what is important. Refer to chapter 11 as you begin to choose from your exercise options. Don't put it off. Being free of smoking is the single most important thing you can do for your health, and a good exercise program is a close second.

REMEMBER: IT IS POSSIBLE TO BREAK THE ADDICTION *AND* THE HABIT

The physical addiction to nicotine is relatively easy to break. It might take a week to eliminate the nicotine from your body after you have truly broken free. Drinking lots of water and fruit juices will alleviate physical symptoms of withdrawal. Relaxation techniques and exercise, covered in chapters 10 and 11, are essential to your transition from smoking as a way of life to freedom from cigarettes.

Psychological Addiction Is More Challenging

Both conscious and unconscious responses to psychological triggers have become automatic for you. Therefore, you can expect certain triggers, such as ringing phones, getting in your car, or good or bad news, to stimulate cravings even months after you have stopped smoking. This means that the victory is not won in a single battle, but at the end of a well-thought-out and relentless war.

The support of friends, family, and people who have successfully stopped smoking will give you vital help after your break-free day. You will want to create a network of people who will offer you encouragement and support when your cravings are particularly strong. And the person you choose as your pal for this program is especially important in sustaining your determination to be free.

46

NOW IS THE TIME
TO PIN DOWN A SUPPORT GROUP

There are bound to be support groups for people in your community who are stopping smoking. In addition to Nicotine Anonymous, there are groups offered through the American Lung Association, the American Cancer Society, and local hospitals. Look for support-group listings in your local newspaper. If none of these sources are fruitful, call the Alcoholics Anonymous hot line about resources for addiction control in your area.

You may want to contact one of the organizations below for more information about breaking free from smoking or to find a support group in your area.

Nicotine Anonymous
http://
www.nicotine-anonymous.org

(This site lists support groups in your area and provides other sources of help.)

American Heart Association National Center
7272 Greenville Avenue
Dallas, TX 75231
(214) 373-6300
1-800-242 8721

(You will be referred to the AHA offices in your area.)

American Cancer Society
1599 Clifton Road, NE
Atlanta, GA 30329
(404) 320-3333
1-800-ACS-2345

(You will be referred to support groups and hospitals in your area.)

American Lung Association
1740 Broadway, 16th Floor
New York, NY 10019-4274
(212) 315-8700
1-800-LUNG-USA

National Cancer Institute
Building 31, Room 10A24
9000 Rockville Pike
Bethesda, MD 20894
(301) 496-5583
1-800-496-5583

Office on Smoking and Health Centers for Disease Control and Prevention
Mail Stop K-50
4770 Buford Highway, NE
Atlanta, GA 30341-3724
1-800-CDC-1311

47

If all else fails, create a support group of your own. You will find that after a while you no longer need support in overcoming nicotine addiction. Time weakens the brain's nicotine receptors, and most former smokers can go days without thinking about a cigarette. However, if you are free for a long time and succumb to the notion that it would be all right to have "just one puff," all your hard work could be lost in a minute. To borrow an adage from AA, "One Puff Is Too Many and Ten Thousand Is Not Enough."

THE URGE WILL GO AWAY . . .

Remember this during the next few weeks: *The urge will go away —whether you smoke or not.*

This simple truth may seem obvious, but dedicated smokers can't believe it. You may have an urge so intense that you think it could only be satisfied with a cigarette. However, if you wait it out, breathe deeply, drink a glass of water, and move around, the urge will go away. Of course, it may frequently return until your body and brain have adjusted to the fact that the supply has been cut off permanently. If you smoke, the urge will certainly go away; but it will also go away if you exert a little energy and resist it.

48

THE NIGHT BEFORE BREAK-FREE DAY

To ensure smooth sailing on your break-free day, do some preparation the night before. First, be sure you have healthful snack foods in your refrigerator. Then go back to the visualization exercises mentioned earlier in this chapter and set up a tentative schedule for the entire first day of your new life. Write down your visualization of how this day will go. It might be something like this:

1. I will rise at 7:30 A.M.
2. I will brush my teeth, get dressed, and go outside for a short walk to greet the day. I will do a short Metta meditation (see chapter 10).

3. After breakfast I will exercise for half an hour. I will be sure to drink lots of water—at least 2 quarts over the course of the day.

4. My pal and I will have lunch together and talk about how I'm doing. I'll go over any difficulties I have had and explain how I handled the urges.

5. In the afternoon I will plan a fun activity: go to a movie, go for a swim, take time to phone family and friends, take a nap, or get a massage.

6. I will go out to dinner with my pal or another friend. After dinner I will go for a walk.

7. I will be careful about what I eat and drink so as to minimize the urge to smoke.

8. I will stay in touch with my feelings all day. If I feel like crying or laughing, I'll go for it. This will help me release the stress that has built up in my body.

You've done all you can to prepare; your mind will control the situation from now on. A wonderful, bright woman who is eternally grateful that she became free of cigarettes said with great conviction, "That little white thing was controlling my life completely and it didn't even have a brain."

49

Break Free

The day has arrived, and you are now officially free of smoking. You started your day with your resolve to be free. You have planned your day and chosen strategies that will carry you through from morning to night.

You may have tried many times before to break free of smoking. I like to think of past failures as stepping-stones to success. However, I have known many people who were as willing and able to follow the program on their first attempt as those who had tried several times before.

The simple truth is that the only failure is the failure to try again.

TAPERING-OFF STRATEGIES

You have probably been tapering off for at least a week. Get out your notebook and jot down what worked for you during this period. Write in the margins if you have to. Was it easy to smoke without a cup of coffee—or vice versa? Were you able to limit the places and times you smoked? Whatever you found beneficial, stick with it now.

The thought that you are about to break free and can never have another cigarette can be daunting. Ignore this thought; instead, keep in mind that you are free right now, and continue to choose to be free right now. It's true that you might smoke again someday. Right now, however, you choose to be free of cigarettes and are prepared for a few withdrawal symptoms.

THREE PRIMARY WITHDRAWAL
SYMPTOMS ON BREAK-FREE DAY

The first withdrawal symptom is extreme fatigue. While this may not set in right away, you should let yourself relax when it does. You have begun the struggle to keep your body in balance, and you truly deserve the time to recover.

The second symptom is a feeling of spaciness. Your brain is finally getting a full dose of oxygen, the chemical that cigarettes impeded. As the carbon monoxide in your blood disappears, the clean oxygen slowly takes back its place in your blood cells, and your brain becomes crystal clear once again.

The third symptom, of course, is simply wanting a cigarette. You can handle that. You know and believe that *the urge will go away whether you smoke or not.*

STRATEGIES TO DEAL WITH
URGES ON BREAK-FREE DAY

1. *Breathe deeply.* Practice lying down with your hands on your abdomen so you will know if the breath is going to the farthest reaches of your lungs. Breathe deeply and observe your hands rising and falling. As a smoker, you have not been able to take a truly deep breath for some time. Practice the refreshment and satisfaction that comes from filling the lungs with a full dose of oxygen. See chapter 10 for more information about breathing.

2. *Drink copious amounts of water.* Keep a water bottle with you at all times; every time you think you want a cigarette, take a sip. You may want to buy a bottle holster to make this more convenient.

3. *Move.* This doesn't necessarily mean exercise, but simply moving from one place to another. Even pacing back and forth can be comforting. If you continue moving in one direction for five or ten minutes, you will find that you are more relaxed and that the urge has gone away.

53

TRY A LIQUID DIET
FOR THE FIRST DAY

Chapter 9 discusses the importance of watching what you eat while you are going through the withdrawal process. If you are at home and have lots of fruits and vegetables and a blender or juicer at hand, discover how refreshed you will feel following a liquid diet for the first day. You can drink the juices frequently during the day and have as many calories as you need and want.

Following are a few blender recipes for easy-to-make, tempting smoothies that will ensure that you won't be hungry and that will be easy on your body.

54

Reeses Cup Smoothie

½ cup peanut butter

1 cup milk

1 tablespoon chocolate syrup

Blend until smooth.

Banana-Strawberry Smoothie

2 large bananas

1 cup strawberries

2 cups ice

Blend and serve and enjoy the crunchiness.

Fruit Slurry

    2 cups any fruit
    2 cups ice

Puree.

Power Aid

    1 cup plain yogurt
    ¼ cup honey
    ½ cup strawberries
    ½ cup honeydew
    nuts (optional)

Blend.

THE ANSWER IS EXERCISE

The day after the participants in my program break free of smoking, I tell them that the answer to every question I ask should be "exercise."

The reason movement is so important is its relationship to the stress response. Putting your body in motion is a signal to your brain and nervous system that you are handling the situation.

Smoking handled only one stressor for you, the need for another cigarette. Now when you feel that urge, you know that it will go away whether you smoke or not. It is also, however, a signal to get moving.

You will need a plan to exercise regularly and often during the first few days after you have broken free of smoking. With exercise, you will be much more able to cope with the many other stressors that may arise.

The exercise strategies you plan are extremely important. Check to see if any of the following activities are available to you today:

- Swimming
- Walking in pleasant surroundings
- Bicycling
- Stretching
- Walking on a treadmill
- Dancing

Add other exercise options to your life that you can truly enjoy. I recently led a stretch class that my wonderful stepdaughter attended. She confessed that she hated to exercise, but she absolutely loved the class. The big difference was the routine I created, in which people could work at their own levels and still feel competent. So concentrate on how you like your body to feel, and find an exercise component that is not too difficult or boring.

When the body is in motion, the brain is better able to sort out what is important. At this point in your life, being free of smoking is the most important benefit you can give to your body, mind, and spirit.

Don't underestimate the significance of what you have done. You should treat yourself as if you have gone through major surgery. You can ask family, friends, and coworkers to cut you some slack if the going gets tough. Tell them that you might be tired or depressed. If the stress builds up when you're at work, duck out to a place of peace and serenity where you can measure the joys of being free of smoking. If you were to go to work two days after an appendectomy, you would get sympathy. Your "cig-arectomy" should get the same kind of attention, especially since you must continue to reward yourself at every stage of recovery.

Remember that you are not a bad person becoming good; you are a sick person becoming well. As soon as the toxins leave your body, if you pay attention, you will notice major healing of your body on a daily basis.

57

OPTIMAL EXPERIENCE: THE ESSENCE OF FLOW

Even though you will endure some trying days, you can trans-form this into a positive and powerful experience. In 1991, the book *Flow: The Psychology of Optimal Experience,* by Mihaly Csikszentmihalyi, appeared on the market as the ultimate self-help book. This was the first book that explained for the layperson the scientific study of happiness. Although it may be hard to believe, you can look at the process of becoming free of smoking as an "optimal experience."

An optimal experience depends on the ability to control what happens in your consciousness moment by moment. Each person has to achieve it on the basis of her own individual efforts and creativity. We all have experienced times when, instead of being buffeted by forces outside ourselves, we feel in control of our actions—masters of our own fate. When this happens, we feel a sense of exhilaration and enjoyment that we cherish. Such experiences show you what life should be like. They come not in passive, relaxed times, but rather when your body or mind is stretched to its limits in an effort to accomplish something difficult and worthwhile.

Another key element of an optimal experience is that it is an end in itself. You can transform any pain you have in breaking free of cigarettes into an experience that reaffirms again and again the control you have gained over your life.

If you're wondering what you will do with all the free time you will have after you stop smoking, read *Flow*.

VISUALIZATION

Visualization is a powerful way to get your mind to focus on the task at hand. There are many accounts of people who have survived difficult situations by turning bleak conditions into controllable experiences. In *The Psychology of Winning*, Denis Waitley tells the story of a pilot who was imprisoned in North Vietnam for seven years. He lost 80 pounds and much of his health during his time in solitary confinement. Upon his release, one of his first requests was to play golf. To the great astonishment of his fellow officers and golf pros, he played at his four handicap despite his emaciated condition. He explained that every day for seven years he had imagined himself playing eighteen holes of golf, carefully choosing his clubs and systematically varying the course. This discipline not only helped preserve his sanity, but apparently also kept his physical skills well honed. He said, "I never three-putted a hole in all my seven years."

You can use this method, too: Visualize yourself in all your old haunts and environments without a cigarette.

PLAY

Among the videos in my documentary collection is Dr. Elaine Goodheart's *Laugh Your Way to Health*. It is a very funny film in which Dr. Goodheart convincingly describes how play and laughter are essential to health. Schedule some play and laughter into the next few days. Rent a funny film or read a good comic novel. Whatever gets you laughing is fine.

59

REWARDS ARE WELCOME

Start to think of the rewards that becoming free of smoking will bestow upon you. The most valuable, of course, are your health and well-being, but there are things that money can buy, such as a weekly massage, a night out with a good friend, or a piece of jewelry that you thought was too expensive when your money was going toward cigarettes. It is very important for you to reward yourself for taking this major, difficult step in your life. Many people put cash aside every day so they can see how much they are saving by not smoking. Put aside the price of one pack of cigarettes right now; do this daily and watch the bounty grow.

WHAT ABOUT THE PATCH, GUM, OR SPRAY?

One of the most frequent questions I am asked is, "What about using a nicotine patch, the nicotine gum, or the newly FDA–approved nasal spray?" Many people think that these items will be useful in dealing with withdrawal symptoms.

In a clinical setting, the use of these methods is called "nicotine replacement therapy." My feeling is that taking these "medications" follows the general pattern of our health care delivery system. I am not convinced that using the patch or gum is any more effective than eating a high-alkaline diet, exercising, and meditating. Of course, I am aware that these crutches have helped many people to eventually break free of cigarettes, so I don't discount them. On the other hand, at least three people who have gone through my program became addicted to the gum, and their withdrawal from it was as difficult as others' withdrawal from cigarettes.

Replacing the nicotine in the body with a device other than cigarettes is just an attempt to treat some of the symptoms of withdrawal. It does not address the nature of addiction, nor does it give your strong, passionate motivation to be free a chance to prevail. Nasal spray, gum, or the patch are passive cures. The medical profession is clearly still looking for the magic bullet that will take care of a complicated addiction.

The Agency for Health Care Policy and Research (AHCPR), a government body, sponsored a nongovernmental panel to make recommendations on smoking cessation. The panel has published a wealth of information for smoking cessation specialists and several guideline pamphlets to help smokers quit.

This material emphasizes the use of the nicotine patch and nicotine gum. *Clinical Practice Guideline #18—Smoking Cessation*, a U.S. Department of Health and Human Services publication, asserts that "pharmacotherapy in the form of nicotine patch or nicotine gum therapy consistently increases smoking cessation rates regardless of the level of adjuvant behavioral or psychosocial interventions. Therefore, its use should be encouraged."

I can't help thinking that if the patch or gum worked for you, you wouldn't be reading this book. I know that it hasn't been the answer to breaking free for hundreds of people who still smoke even though they have a medicine cabinet full of these expensive products. I do, however, believe that medical intervention is necessary for those who are clinically depressed and find that stopping smoking makes it worse.

It is important to realize that nobody can do it alone. Whatever your belief system, muster all your forces to help you stay the course of freedom from nicotine. Sustain your belief in yourself. Repeat a meaningful affirmation or prayer every time you have a strong desire to smoke. In chapter 10, there is a long list of affirmations that you can say out loud or think silently. You can choose one or two prayers that will help you maintain an inner message of hope. I personally like to hear people say, "I love being free of smoking."

61

Withdrawal

CHANGES TO THE MIND AND BODY

There are many proven techniques to help you calm your mind while your body goes through the dramatic changes of becoming free of cigarettes. You are experiencing a wide range of emotions and now is the time to use your arsenal of positive techniques to help you accept the present and be ready for the time when you will be completely free of even the thought of cigarettes.

Keep in mind a few techniques that have proved effective: deep breathing, meditation, and positive affirmations.

Kathy's story illustrates the amount of energy it may take you to go through the early stages of withdrawal. During one of my Break Free sessions we noticed that Kathy had not been seen for some time. Fearing the worst, we waited patiently for her to show up at the evening meeting. When asked what she had been doing all day, she replied simply, "I was very busy up in my room all afternoon—not smoking."

Many smokers have exaggerated notions of the agony of going without cigarettes and want to know how long they will be affected by withdrawal symptoms. Since physiology varies widely among individuals, the answer has a lot to do with your attitude about the process. On average, it takes two to three days for the nicotine level in your body to drop significantly below your maintenance level. During that time you will have frequent urges, which are the most significant symptoms of withdrawal. If you drink lots of water, breathe deeply, and keep moving, you will be able to go long periods of time without being aware of your changed situation.

SYMPTOMS

As you notice the time between urges increasing, you may become aware of some of the physical symptoms of recovery described below. You may feel all, some, or none of these symptoms within the first week. Remember that your body is healing and that over time, the symptoms will abate. Don't worry about them unless they persist for a long time.

Cravings for a Cigarette

Cravings for a cigarette are frequent and intense within the first two to three days after stopping. The cravings become less frequent over the next four or five days, but they may increase again and persist for many weeks. Most former smokers—even those who have been free for many years—still report an occasional urge for a cigarette. Deep breathing and immediate activity will help distract you from your craving. The worst of the cravings usually end within a couple of weeks after breaking free. You know you're in good shape when you no longer think of cigarettes all the time.

Coughing

Your lungs and upper respiratory system are now getting rid of the built-up toxins that restricted your breathing while you were smoking. Your body is cleaning house, so don't panic if you cough or spit up blackish mucus. Your cough should last only a few days; cough drops or syrups may help relieve the symptoms.

Sleeplessness

Smokers lack energy, and their sleep tends to be restless because of coughing and difficult breathing. Now that you are no longer smoking, you are healthier and your body has more energy. You should need fewer hours of sleep, and the sleep you get should be more restful. If you want to sleep longer, use more of your new energy during the day by exercising harder and going to bed later, when you tend to be more tired.

Feeling Sleepy

Some smokers report that they get a boost of energy from smoking. The body needs time to adjust to not having a cigarette every half hour or so. If you feel sleepy, don't hesitate to take a nap during the first few days you are free of smoking. This is why we suggest you break free on a long weekend.

Mouth Sores

A small number of people who stop smoking are affected by chemical changes in their mouths and may suffer minor problems including blisters, sores, and inflammation. For years, your mouth has had to withstand the endless attacks of hot smoke, so it can handle the sores. They'll go away in a few days.

Occasional Dizziness

Because your body is taking in more oxygen through the lungs than you have been used to, you may feel dizzy. These dizzy spells will last only a few seconds. This symptom may recur for four or five days, until your body adjusts to increased oxygen intake.

Constipation

Internal movement may decrease for a brief period when a smoker lowers or stops his cigarette use. This symptom rarely lasts longer than three to four days.

Tightness in the Chest

Some newly free smokers complain of chest pain after stopping. This happens because your body is getting more fresh air than usual. The extra air fills the lungs and makes them feel tighter.

This symptom should last for only a day or two after stopping. See your doctor if it persists.

Irritability

It is the nicotine that causes your addiction to cigarettes. When the nicotine level declines, your body begins to sense the loss. This can cause tension and be symptomatic of the grief process (discussed on pages 68–70). Deep breathing and exercise will help relieve irritability.

Lack of Concentration

Some former smokers notice lapses in concentration soon after they break free. This symptom may be the combined result of other withdrawal symptoms—irritability, sleeplessness, and the change in your routine. Give it time. Your focus will be clearer within a few days, and you will develop new ways of coping without reaching for a cigarette.

Physical Symptoms Not Covered

Remember, not all symptoms that surface after you stop are due to smoking withdrawal. It has already been suggested that you see your dentist soon after stopping smoking. In some cases, periodontal disease may become more evident.

Individuals often report having a severe head cold soon after smoking cessation. One doctor who went through my program speculated that this was due to the absence of the toxic effect nicotine had on bacteria in the mouth and throat.

If any symptom, particularly a persistent cough or extreme fatigue, persists for more than a week or two, it is imperative that you consult your doctor.

THE GRIEF PROCESS

Smokers tend to think about cigarettes in a positive way, sometimes as their best friend. This is indeed a trap, because you know that your dear friend is systematically killing your life force. However, there is no getting away from the fact that you will go through a grief process as part of your withdrawal. The emotional relationship you have had with the little white thing that has controlled your life cannot be minimized.

In the late 1950s, Elizabeth Kübler-Ross analyzed the stages of grief people go through after a major loss. You may not go through all these stages, nor necessarily in the order given, but it is helpful to be aware of where these feelings come from and how to cope with them. Kübler-Ross's six stages of grief are as follows:

1. *Denial.* For some time, you told yourself that you could give up the habit anytime. When you found out this was not true, you probably found examples of older people who had smoked all their lives without any apparent symptoms. You had the comforting thought that you also could go on smoking unscathed.
2. *Bargaining.* Many smokers stop buying cartons and buy cigarettes a pack at a time, promising themselves each time that after they smoke these twenty cigarettes, they

will stop smoking. Or they switch to a "safe" cigarette that's low in tar and nicotine. Though they actually smoke more of these cigarettes than they would their regular brand, they have the illusion of taking care of their health. One brand of cigarettes recently advertised that its tobacco had "no additives." This caused an immediate boost in sales without any further explanation of the significance of the statement.

3. *Anger and strong emotions.* When smokers break free, they can become irritable and angry while going through chemical withdrawal. You may look for someone to blame for your temporary discomfort. In this stage, a clever manipulator can convince several people that the only way to end the anger and noise is for him to go back to smoking. A spouse may even insist that the partner take up smoking again to relieve the overall tension. You've heard this sort of story repeated hundreds of times with variations. The solution is to recognize that this is part of the grieving process and that it will ease off with every day that you get some distance from your break-free day.

4. *Depression and loneliness.* These are powerful feelings that must be addressed. When your positive affirmations have turned into messages of despair and hopelessness, you must reprogram your thinking and recognize that sadness and loneliness are part of life and that you probably had these feelings even when you were smoking. This is the time to share your feelings with supportive people and to understand that

returning to smoking would be the most depressive action you could possibly take.

5. *Guilt.* You may find yourself thinking about the stupidity of being controlled by such a serious addiction. You may wonder if the health consequences are reversible. You may feel guilty for causing your family great concern when you had a smoking-related illness. Such negative thoughts will put you back into depression, so recognize that this is just a stage and be patient. You will get through it.

6. *Hope, reality, and acceptance.* You have arrived at the final stage of healing and you begin to think, "I'm free of smoking and very happy about it," and "I have gone through this difficult time and I am proud that I am now in control of my life."

You may wonder whether you really have to grieve. Grief over the loss of a daily companion, as your cigarettes turned out to be, is a part of the natural human condition and you should expect it as a consequence of your new freedom. Don't fight it. Dare to go through it all even though it is painful. It is healthy in the long run to acknowledge the loss and move on.

LINGERING DEPRESSION

You know yourself better than anyone. If you tend to suffer from mild or chronic depression, you may have used this as an excuse to continue to smoke.

Phoebe was a television executive who came from New York to attend one of the earliest sessions of my Break Free program. Having recently gone through a bout with cancer therapy, her hair was just coming back and she was anxious to follow her doctor's edict that she stop smoking. She heard his command but could not remain free of cigarettes, even after ten return trips to my program. She came two or three times a year, which was beginning to be an embarrassment to me and to her. I was prepared to say, "No, Phoebe, I can't help you," if she returned to the group again.

Serendipitously, she called to tell me that her doctor had put her on an antidepressant medication and that she had not smoked for four months. She had long been concerned with the side effects of medication, but she recognized that depression had thwarted all her previous attempts to break free. She successfully stayed on the prescription for a year until her body stabilized. She is now six years smoke-free.

If your depression continues, it would be a good idea to see a physician. There are many new solutions available, both allopathic and alternative.

71

8

Cravings and Urges

WHAT ARE CRAVINGS?

A craving is a physical as well as psychological symptom of withdrawal that may last longer than the few days it takes to rid your body of nicotine. It is a powerful, screaming urge to smoke.

A craving often feels like hunger, and you'll feel a strong desire to put something in your mouth. As you will see in chapter 12, what you put in your mouth need not be food. I knew a woman in Asia who was told she absolutely had to stop smoking, so she bought a small ivory letter opener—and kept clicking this thing against her teeth. At the time, I was still smoking, and I thought her clicking would drive me crazy, but it drove her to freedom and it took me a long time to catch up.

Cinnamon sticks are effective in satisfying cravings; licorice root does well also. Sunflower seeds pack a double whammy by keeping your mouth occupied and providing supernutrition.

CHANGING ACTIVITIES
WHEN URGES COME

The best defense against cravings is to be prepared. When you feel an urge or craving, choose activities that change how you feel. The three strategies that seem to pay off immediately in killing urges are as the following:

1. Breathe deeply. Smokers have not used their lungs effectively for a long time, so getting a good shot of oxygen is an immediate blow to an urge. (See chapter 10.)
2. Drink more water in a day than you ever have before —at least eight to ten glasses. This helps to flush all the toxins out of your body, and you begin to feel healthier. Keep a water bottle with you at all times during the first week. (See chapter 9.)
3. Move from the place where you feel the urge. You can walk, run, or do a few stretching exercises—just move. (See chapter 11.)

In addition to these three, do at least seven of the following activities a day:

Take a hot shower
Listen to relaxing music

Brush and floss your teeth

Splash cold water on your face

Snap a rubber band worn on your wrist

Hull and eat sunflower seeds

Play with a toothpick, carrot stick, cinnamon stick, or celery stick

Telephone a friend as often as you want

Go swimming or soak in a hot tub—or a plain old bathtub

Visit as frequently as you can with supportive, nonsmoking friends

Get up from the table immediately after eating and go for a walk

Keep your juicer going—make interesting concoctions to drink slowly

Chew sugarless gum

Keep eating alkaline foods (see chapter 9)

Take charge of your thoughts and move them away from cigarettes

THE CRAVINGS WILL PASS
WHETHER YOU SMOKE OR NOT

When you have a craving, remember that it will pass within a short time—maybe a minute or two. If it returns, remember that it disappeared the last time and will again. You can time the frequency of urges to see that the period elapsed between them is increasing. Of course, psychological triggers such as finishing a

meal will probably induce a series of urges. Yet I have heard
dozens of people say that once they acknowledged that there
would be discomfort when they broke free of cigarettes, the
urges never happened. You can waste hours worrying about
things that never happen. You won't crawl up the walls, or jump
out of your skin, and you will never come to the point where it
is a life-or-death necessity for you to have a cigarette—unless
you forget the simple truth that has kept thousands of people on
course: *the urge will go away—whether you smoke or not!*

Count your victories in minutes and hours. Look back on
each successful hour as though it were a week in your life. Time
is on your side, but how you spend it is up to you. The power of
thinking positively as you go through these first few hours and
days, feeling that you are victorious over your urges, will help
you enormously in the weeks and months to come.

BREAK THE CHAIN OF CRAVINGS

The following progression illustrates how people who don't deal
positively with cravings can relapse. It could be useful to check
your progress.

1. You have dreams about cigarettes. This is the mildest
   type of craving, but you might be pretty rattled when
   you wake up and remember the dream. You may feel
   that you are slipping in your resolve to be free.
2. You have more conscious thoughts about smoking,
   and you go back frequently to the rhetorical question,

"Wouldn't it be nice if I could relax with a cigarette?"
This may be just a quick thought, but it leaves you
with the question unanswered, ready to pop up again.

3. Intrusive thoughts come into your consciousness
   when you are otherwise occupied. Out of the blue,
   you get a thought of how great it would be to visit
   your old friend—cigarettes.

4. You engage in inner arguments with yourself about
   whether or not to have a cigarette. You think, "I'll just
   have one—no problem."

5. You may not be able to keep cigarettes out of your
   daydreams. You might start thinking fondly of the
   pleasures of smoking, remembering only the good
   times.

6. You fall into a pattern of thinking obsessively of your
   need for nicotine, and it is very hard to change your
   thoughts. Dwelling on all or some of the above five
   links in the chain of cravings indicates that you are in
   real danger.

7. You begin to plot—perhaps half consciously: How
   might I do it? When will I be alone? Will someone
   give me a cigarette? How will I get a light? How
   could I hide the smell?

8. You become so convinced that you are about to
   relapse that you have withdrawal-like sensations,
   feeling as if you just had a cigarette and are suffering
   from the effects.

9. Finally, you surrender to relapse.

Follow the 3 Rs to interrupt the chain of cravings:

1. *Recognize* that it is a craving—before it escalates into a "panic attack."
2. *Reduce* the craving—use deep breathing, drink water, exercise, use relaxation techniques, and follow sensible nutrition. Talk to someone who has recently broken free. You will find that others are going through cravings too. Remember: Silence is the enemy of recovery.
3. *Refocus*—focus your energy on your recovery program. Motivate yourself with positive thoughts. Going through cravings doesn't mean you are going to relapse. Get rid of guilt and doubt and put that energy back into your program. Avoid thinking that the phone would weigh 100 pounds if you picked it up to ask for help. Call your pal or another friend to tell her of your difficulties, and listen to her suggestions.

Learn the Causes of Cravings

Following are some of the likely causes for your cravings, beyond the physiological need for nicotine:

- *Euphoric recall.* We only remember the early, good times of the addiction. We do not remember the painful or embarrassing parts.

- *Environmental triggers.* Plan to stay away from your old haunts as much as possible. Make an effort to change your social situation until you feel safe.
- *Mood-altering drugs.* Be careful with substances that can cause rapid fluctuations in your feelings—including caffeine, sleeping pills, alcohol, and sugar. Don't self-medicate, and watch your diet.

Pinpoint your own causes, and deal with them.

Nutrition

THE FOOD YOU EAT HELPS
STAY THE COURSE TO FREEDOM

You will need all the tools I can offer to remain smoke-free through the next few days and months. Early in my career helping people deal with nicotine addiction, I spoke with a holistic doctor who told me about research on how smokers can use nutrition to manage their addiction. In his book *A Distinctive Approach to Psychological Research,* Stanley Schachter, Ph.D., writes that eating alkaline foods minimizes withdrawal symptoms and maximizes the ability to stay free of nicotine. Dr. Schachter bases this conclusion on his own extensive research.

WITHDRAWAL SYMPTOMS
AND HOMEOSTASIS

A great deal of research has been done concerning the body's chemical balance and withdrawal symptoms. Your body is always working to be in chemical and physiological balance—the wonderful state of *homeostasis,* defined as "the tendency to maintain, or the maintenance of normal, internal stability in an organism by coordinated responses of the organ systems that automatically compensate for environmental changes." Do you ever think about how amazingly well all the systems of your body—including body temperature, heart rate, blood pressure, and the endocrine system—work together in harmony to keep everything operating more or less in balance? When you look at the spectrum of illnesses, you realize that medical science centers on just one goal: keeping the body in balance, or homeostasis.

As a smoker, you were always on the brink of a serious medical condition because your body was struggling to be in balance. I think of smokers as walking around off-center, leaning to one side like the pendulum of a clock stuck at its outermost limit. As you become free of nicotine, the pendulum will begin to swing gently again, and your state of health will soon reflect the balanced rhythm of a healthy human being.

Your health depends upon the acid-base equilibrium of the blood. Any form of illness indicates a disturbed state of body chemistry—generally an acid state. Therefore, when disease is present the acid condition must be corrected as quickly as possible to restore the proper base, or alkalinity, to the body. This should be done with *food*—not drugs. Foods are the only wholesome alkalizers. They are intended by nature to keep the alkaline reserve of the body at the high level conducive to buoyant health.

TESTING THE ALKALINITY THEORY

When I learned about Dr. Schachter's theory that having a pre-dominantly alkaline system makes it easier to stop using tobacco, I tested how alkaline foods would affect withdrawal symptoms in the participants of my residential smoking cessation program. All members of the group were served a high-alkaline diet for the seven-day initial process of ridding the body of nicotine. Most smokers fear this first week of withdrawal, but my test confirmed that it can be almost free of negative symptoms when attention is paid to the food that is consumed.

Dr. Schachter's research showed that the more acidic your body's chemical balance, the faster you flush nicotine out of your system. You might think you would want to be free of nicotine quickly, but the nicotine should leach out of your body slowly, so the urges will not rush back.

According to Dr. Schachter, the remedy for withdrawal symptoms is to maximize alkaline foods. He tested his theory that the more alkaline you are, the less you will feel the need to smoke in order to maintain a comfort level of nicotine in your blood. Dr. Schachter theorizes that stress, alcohol, and acidic foods can rapidly drain your supply of nicotine. The researchers also found a correlation between emotion and acidity: students under stress had highly acidic urine, as did people who were depressed or angry.

Do people smoke because of anxiety, or is it the acidic chemistry in their bodies caused by this anxiety that produces the cravings for cigarettes? In one study, students were given highly alkaline bicarbonate of soda, and the professor conducting the study made an amazing discovery: as acid levels were reduced, so was the urge to smoke. This seems to explain why people want

83

to smoke more in the morning: "It's the body's natural rhythm to be more acidic after it has slept," writes Dr. Schachter.

"Any kind of physiological factor can be important in determining smoking behavior," Dr. Schachter states in his book. His experiments with teenagers, for example, showed that those with acidic urine were more likely to smoke than those with alkaline urine. After a five-week group therapy session designed to help adults stop smoking, it was discovered that 82 percent who had failed were "acidic."

WHAT FOODS ARE
THE BEST ALKALIZERS?

84

The best alkalizers are vegetables, and the worst are meat and alcohol. There are no alkalizers that compare with fresh, raw juices. Fruit juices are often more palatable, but vegetable juices are more potent.

Limes, lemons, and even grapefruits are not acid forming. The organic acids that these and many other fruits contain are burned off by the body during metabolism. The end product, referred to as ash, is alkaline. It may be strange to think of a steak, lamb chop, or chicken breast as an acid-forming food, but the fact is that they, like other sources of protein, produce acidic end products, specifically phosphoric acid and sulfuric acid.

Following are five simple principles that can shift your diet in the alkaline direction and serve as a guideline as you are breaking free of cigarettes:

1. Go very easy on meat, poultry, and eggs.
2. Eat a lot of vegetables and fruits.

3. Get plenty of milk, milk products, or soy substitutes.
   These are all base forming.
4. Go somewhat lightly on breads and cereals.
5. Avoid seafood except for shrimp and all whitefish.

The question of how to achieve the best acid-base balance does not, unfortunately, have a simple, acid-or-alkaline answer. Still, it is important to make a significant move in the alkaline direction. If you are accustomed to eating a lot of red meat, poultry, or fish and not much in the way of vegetables or fruit, you probably have acidic urine. Changing your food intake enough so that your urine is less acidic and more alkaline really counts when you are addressing nicotine withdrawal. It also counts as far as general health is concerned. After you accomplish the mighty feat of breaking free of smoking, you will have the time to think about continuing a healthy pattern of food consumption.

What happens if acid-forming foods and base foods are exactly balanced? The urine will still be on the acid side, because the body's metabolism tends to produce an acid surplus.

What Could Be Easier Than Juice Therapy?

When I was a child, Gaylord Hauser was a household name around my home. My mother had his book *You Are What You Eat* in our kitchen. Many years later I realized that Hauser's words had profoundly affected my thinking. Hauser pioneered raw-juice therapy in America and explained the advantages of juice over whole vegetables or fruit: "Fruit and vegetable juices, because of their concentrated goodness, are the quickest means of revitalizing the body. It is also true that you can balance the chemicals and revitalize the body with whole fresh fruits and vegetables, but you cannot do so as quickly as you can with the juices. In fact, it would be almost impossible to eat enough fruit and vegetables to get the minerals and vitamins found in a quart of juices. The bulk and roughage would be too filling, too cumbersome for our digestive and elimination systems to handle."

Carrot juice has been established as the best rapid alkalizer, partly because it is processed efficiently by the body, and partly because it can generally be consumed in large quantities without unpleasant or harmful effects. Acid stomachs respond quickly to carrot juice, as does "acid mouth," which produces bleeding gums and "pink toothbrush." Having served carrot juice for many years, I have found that there is no middle ground in people's reactions. Either you think it is a fantastic new experience or you shudder and push it away like a two-year-old.

Other vegetable juices, such as celery, cucumber, lettuce, and cabbage, are also valuable alkalizers, as are the various fruit juices. Your stomach may sometimes have difficulty handling excessive quantities of acid fruits, especially when the stomach lining is inflamed and irritated. Under these circumstances, vegetable juices, which are more bland, should be used for alkalinization.

The key point to remember is this: Any shift in the alkaline direction helps lower your cravings and minimizes withdrawal symptoms when you break free of cigarettes.

SUNFLOWER SEEDS
VERSUS NICOTINE

Sunflower seeds are an excellent source of vital nutrients. They contain most of the B vitamins, vitamin E, and many essential fatty acids. Pound for pound, they contain twice as much iron and twenty-five times as much thiamin (a B vitamin) as steak. Research has shown that sunflower seeds are particularly good for people trying to wean themselves from cigarettes.

A participant in one of my early smoking cessation programs was William Bennett, then the director of the Office of National Drug Control Policy. I remember him telling me that for the first two months after he became free of his three-pack-a-day habit, he always had a handful of sunflower seeds in his pocket. His assistant said his office looked like a birdcage.

Clinical studies have proved that carrying raw or shelled sunflower seeds is beneficial to would-be nonsmokers. Every time you feel the desire to smoke, it is suggested that you go through the process of breaking seeds open and popping them into your mouth to munch on until the desire subsides. In a few weeks, the desire to smoke seems to fade. How can this David and Goliath effect be explained—the humble sunflower seed versus the ogre nicotine?

Sunflower seeds contain compounds that mimic some of the effects of nicotine and can offer smokers some of the gratification they seek. Nicotine tends to have a mildly soothing sedative effect on the nervous system; so do sunflower seeds, which contain various sedative essential oils and plenty of B vitamins, which are always good for the nerves. Nicotine triggers the release of glycogen from the liver, producing a temporary increase in brain activity; sunflower seeds produce a similar lift. Nicotine raises the level of adrenal hormones in the body; sunflower seeds also stimulate the adrenal glands. Sunflower seeds are healthful and nonallergic, and they effectively break through the smoker's pattern of addiction.

WATER: THE MEDIUM OF LIFE

We have already thoroughly discussed how eating the right food helps you break free of cigarettes with a minimum of symptoms, and we know that following a well-balanced diet is an important element in our overall health and well-being. However, we sometimes forget the other critical element of sound nutrition: water.

Everything in our bodies occurs in a water medium. We can go without food for two months or more, but without water we can only survive a few days. Yet most people have no idea how much water they should be drinking. In fact, many Americans live from day to day in a dehydrated state. This is particularly true of smokers, who often interpret thirst or hunger as a need for a cigarette.

The Physiology of Water

Dr. Albert Szent-Györgyi, the discoverer of vitamin C, said, "There is no life without water. . . . Water is part and parcel of living machinery. Without water, we'd be poisoned to death by our own waste products and toxins resulting from metabolism."

When the kidneys remove wastes from our bodies, the wastes must be dissolved in water. If there isn't enough water, wastes are not removed effectively and damage to the kidneys may result. Water is vital to digestion and metabolism, and most weight-reduction diets include drinking eight to ten glasses of water a day. Water helps to regulate our body temperature through perspiration, and it also lubricates our joints.

Our lungs need water to facilitate the intake of oxygen and the exhalation of carbon dioxide. Just by exhaling, we dispense approximately a pint of water a day. We've discussed elsewhere how smokers put their entire pulmonary systems at risk. Now that you are going through the process of freedom from smoking, healing will progress rapidly in every part of your body just by adding significantly to your water consumption. If you drink enough water to be in "fluid balance," as doctors describe it, you can begin to repair all of your body's physiological functions that have been endangered by smoking.

In one of my early programs, I invited a doctor to speak to the group about the importance of drinking water to carry away the toxins provided by smoking. Several people in the group were on diuretics and felt that they shouldn't increase their water consumption. The doctor had to explain the paradox that if you're not drinking enough water, your body starts retaining water to compensate for this shortage. The way to eliminate fluid retention is to drink more water—not less.

People breaking free of smoking should drink at least ten 8-ounce glasses a day. You need to drink even more if you are overweight, exercise a lot, or live in a hot climate.

Your water intake should be spaced throughout the day, including the evening. No more than four glasses per hour is recommended. You may think that drinking so much water will have you constantly running to the bathroom, but though the bladder may be hypersensitive when water intake is first increased, it will adjust after a couple of weeks, and and you will urinate less frequently in larger amounts.

Water versus Other Beverages

Now we come to one of my pet peeves: the idea that soda pop counts as a beverage. I believe that like smoking, the overconsumption of soft drinks is a national health disaster.

There is a big difference between pure water and beverages that *contain* water. Biochemically, water is water—obviously, it's present in fruit juice, soft drinks, beer, coffee, and tea. Unfortunately, while these drinks do contain water, they also contain substances that negate water's positive effects.

Beer contains water, but it also contains alcohol, which is a toxic substance. Caffeinated beverages such as tea and coffee adversely affect the adrenal glands, while fruit juices contain a lot of sugar, which is hard on the pancreas. Diet sodas, though, are the worst. They contain high levels of sodium, aspartame, caffeine, and artificial flavorings, and they tax the body much more than the water they contain can cleanse it. Another problem with these beverages is that you lose your taste for water and have to retrain your brain to enjoy the flavor of pure water.

The bottom line is that the daily water intake I've recommended means just that—*water.*

10

Relaxation

TREAT YOURSELF TO A MASSAGE

Think of the benefits of massage as part of your recovery program. Massage is not a hedonistic indulgence; on the contrary, it has many health-enhancing effects, not the least of which is to help eliminate some of the four thousand chemicals cigarettes have deposited in your joints and muscles. A relaxing, therapeutic massage will help you through the first stages of withdrawal from smoking. Since you'll be saving a good deal of money by not buying cigarettes, what better way to reward yourself than arranging for regular massages? Contact the local massage school in your area for a recommendation of a massage therapist (or get an excellent massage from a therapist-in-training at a discounted price). Most health clubs have a massage therapist on staff, as do many chiropractors.

MEDITATION

As the director of a health spa, I receive many applications from eager young people who want to be in the health field. One letter in particular sparked my curiosity; it was from a young man who graduated first in his class from a well-regarded high school and then graduated from an Ivy League college. Why would he want to teach yoga and meditation at a resort?

When we met, I was instantly impressed with his youth and maturity, and he became a most valuable presence in the company. I learned from him how to describe meditation so it would be seen as beneficial, not shrouded in mysticism, by the people in my programs. He has since moved on, but I am grateful for his insights into the simplicity of meditation, and I have adapted his explanations to fit your needs as you go through the process of becoming free.

I'll explain what deep meditation is and what it is not, how to meditate, and the benefits of meditation. Meditation does not mean thinking about problems over and over, with increased stress and anxiety. It is quite possible that you have addressed the possibility of breaking free of cigarettes by going over the negatives and positives endlessly but coming to no resolution. This is not meditation. This is obsession, and we smokers know how easy it can be to obsess over the loss of cigarettes.

Meditation does not mean thinking about a problem or gathering insights into the deeper meanings of any issue. This is actually contemplation. And when you sit around doing nothing, just letting your mind go wherever it drifts, you are daydreaming or relaxing, not meditating.

Meditation doesn't have to have any mystical connotation. It is simply the practice of noticing when the mind wanders, when it moves away from a chosen point of focus. Any point of focus, or anchor, you choose can help you get into a meditative state. You can use a word (mantra) or music or color—anything that your mind can return to in a relaxed state. Practicing meditation is another way of using your mind to enhance your body.

Since you are concentrating on becoming free of smoking, and maintaining that freedom, you should choose an anchor or affirmation that supports your new role as a non-smoking person.

Remember, anchors must be "in the now." Several positive affirmations are offered on page 98; for now, let's concentrate on just one. When you start to meditate, say this to yourself:

93

I am free of smoking.

You can understand how affirmations work by considering the process of training a dog to sit. You tell the dog, "Sit," as you push him down. When he wanders off, you drag him back and go through the process again, telling him again and again to sit. He finally gets the message and sits when you tell him to. Your mind is like an untrained dog, constantly wandering off in all directions. Leading the mind back to an anchor that is positive or absolutely neutral helps to keep you locked into the present time. Don't worry about how long you stay on your anchor or affirmation. Turn your interfering thoughts into little sailboats and let them sail off into the sea.

Set the Stage to Meditate

To begin your meditation, you should be seated in a relaxed position with your spine as straight as possible. I personally find it more comfortable to lie on my back if I am going to stay immobile while meditating. There is some danger of falling asleep, which is not meditation, but if you are on a hard surface, this is not likely. Just be sure you can relax your body as you begin to relax your mind.

First, listen to the quietness around you. Release your mind to your anchor. *Om,* which means "one," is a typical mantra in certain systems of meditation, but it really doesn't matter what you say. The only condition in choosing an affirmation, word, or sound is to be sure that you resist the temptation of making any judgments about what you are repeating in your mind. As you release your mind to dwell on the anchor, notice when you drift off; when this happens, return to your anchor. Stay with this practice for five minutes the first time, then increase it to fifteen minutes of quiet meditation.

The Benefits of Meditation

There are both practical and spiritual benefits of meditation. If you are wondering whether the practice is for you, consider that meditating helps us manage stress by focusing on the *process* of the events in our lives, rather than the results.

A good example of focusing on the process would be your thoughts and actions as you plan a party for people you want to impress. You begin by agonizing over when to have the party, whom to invite, and what the menu should be. You then wonder if the people you invite will like this or that combination of guests and food. Finally, you make your decisions and start the actual work of cooking. With all the party elements in front of you, you may still be nervous and doubtful about whether the outcome will be pleasing to the guests.

Instead of worrying about the whole party, do one thing at a time: take the ingredients out of the refrigerator and start chopping, set the table, arrange the seating, and check everything off your list. Keep all your activities "in the now," and you will most likely find that going through the process will be a relaxing experience. By not worrying about what people might think and concentrating on the step-by-step method you followed to achieve your goal, you will probably get the results you want.

This idea of concentrating on the process rather than the results can be applied to other activities in your life, such as working, writing a book, planting a garden, or taking a trip. As Ben Cohen of Ben & Jerry's ice cream fame said, "If it's not fun, why do it?"

Meditation Will Help You Get "Unstuck"

Most smokers get stuck in their efforts to become free of smoking by concentrating on the pain they think will result from giving up cigarettes. They worry and struggle with the idea that they'll be forced to never have another cigarette, when instead they can *choose* not to have a cigarette—one urge at a time.

By repeating "I love being free of cigarettes" over and over, you emphasize the positives of your present freedom as opposed to the dreariness of your former addiction, and you avoid the trap of feeling sorry for yourself.

Improved Decision Making Through Meditation

Another practical benefit of meditation relates to the "fight or flight," or stress, response. In an emergency, or when we sense danger, our bodies go into a heightened state of readiness. Blood pressure and heart rate increase, blood rushes to the muscles for increased strength, and no energy is wasted on the digestive or reproductive systems. Everyone can recall an incident when the stress response kicked in to make us more alert during a crisis.

On the other hand, we often react to imagined dangers as if they were real, and go through the whole stress response, beating up on ourselves for no good reason. Meditation can defuse this feeling of danger. In becoming free of smoking, you can switch your mind from this habitual response and remember that you have chosen to be free of cigarettes and are simply going through some anxiety. Meditation can rest your mind as you pull it back to the anchor.

Let's say you're thinking about your desire for a cigarette. Your mind may drift toward the thought of deprivation, but you can readjust your thinking and choose to stay with your decision to be free of cigarettes. When you notice the stress response beginning, breathe deeply, drink lots of water, move your body to a different location, or just move in place. Choose to stay free of cigarettes. Use frequent, short meditations in place of nicotine to deal with stress.

Spiritual Benefits of Meditation

When we slow down, we can appreciate more of the beauty of our surroundings and have a greater reverence for life. Think of traveling down a freeway at ninety miles per hour. You see only a blur at that rate, and even when you slow down to fifty all the sights along the road are whizzing right by. When you get down to fifteen miles per hour, you begin to notice the mountains, trees, animals, and people along the way. And when you walk, you can enjoy all the precious details. During meditation, your mind slows down as you return to your anchor and affirm that you appreciate your new freedom from cigarettes and that you value your life and your spiritual beliefs. Following the simple rule of staying focused on your anchor, you can meditate easily and frequently when your mind starts racing.

97

TUNING IN TO AFFIRMATIONS

Affirmations are positive statements that confirm positive actions. A psychologist who participated in one of my programs shared the affirmations he used in his meditation system.

1. Find a quiet place free from interruption and distraction.
2. Systematically relax your body using progressive relaxation.
3. Imagine yourself in a calm, peaceful, serene, and tranquil place.
4. Repeat the affirmations silently to yourself as if they are true for you.
5. Visualize each affirmation with positive images and feelings as you repeat them.

Affirmations to Keep You Free of Smoking

I am calmly and confidently letting go of smoking.

It feels good to let go of cigarettes . . . and to breathe free.

I enjoy breathing only clean, clear air.

It feels good to be taking control of my life by letting go of smoking.

When an urge to smoke occurs, I will take some deep breaths, relax, and let the urge pass me by.

I enjoy acting decisively to let cigarettes fall away from me and pass out of my life.

I am gaining my freedom from smoking now, and I enjoy that freedom.

As I let go of smoking, I feel the power to be more in charge of my life.

I give myself love and respect for letting go of smoking.

I love being free of smoking.

I know that this time will pass, and I will enjoy the freedom of not smoking.

METTA MEDITATION

Metta meditation is a Buddhist practice that recognizes the humanity in you and others. When I stumbled upon this meditation technique, I decided that it was the simplest to teach and one of the most satisfying ways to occupy the mind when you are going through some stress or turbulent thoughts. I practice it almost every day. Seeing the negative people in your life in a positive light brings rewarding peace of mind.

Begin by focusing your mind on affirmations that promote self-love. Then focus your mind on loving people in your life. During this process, it's the intention that's important, not what you feel. As in all forms of meditation, the intention is to relax the mind so it can approach problems and decisions on a different level than the rational mind. The Metta meditation process allows you to direct your mind to float through your relationships with positive, calming affirmations.

According to this practice, cultivating a loving heart toward oneself and others is based on intention, not emotion.

99

How to Do a Metta Meditation

1. Sit comfortably in as quiet an environment as possible. Breathe gently and repeat the following phrases to yourself:

   May I be happy. May I be healthy.
   May I be free from danger. May I live with ease.

   You can choose your own phrases. The idea is to encourage a feeling of friendship and generosity toward yourself and others. In this and the following steps, your mind will wander, so don't worry about how long you actually remain focused on the affirmations or person. The time for each meditation will vary for everyone. As long as you return to the affirmations whenever you are aware that your mind has wandered, you are doing the Metta meditation correctly. Continue for five to ten minutes.

2. Call to mind someone you love or for whom you feel great respect or gratitude. Reflect on his or her goodness, and then repeat the phrases you used earlier, substituting the word *you* for *I*. Try to connect with each phrase, one at a time, without consciously striving to conjure feelings of love. Continue for five minutes.

3. Focus on a neutral person—such as a supermarket cashier or a stranger on the street—or on groups of people, such as flood victims or fellow plane passengers. Repeat the process.

4. Finally, focus on a person who has caused you difficulty or pain. Repeat the affirmations about being happy, healthy, free of danger, and living at ease. You may be able to connect with this person only on the basis of shared humanity. This does not mean you condone the other's behavior in any way, or deny your own pain.

VISUALIZING YOUR SUCCESS

As I wrote in chapter 6, visualization is a powerful tool in winning the war against cigarettes. Most athletes understand the power of visualization. Some Olympic skaters see themselves going through all the rigors of their routines without a flaw. In the same way, you can visualize your daily life without cigarettes. By visualizing your day without cigarettes, from getting up in the morning to going to bed at night, you are engaging your subconscious in this concentrated campaign against smoking.

If possible, try visualization while you lie in bed, either at night or in the morning, with music playing gently in the background. Mentally scan your body, finding any tense spots or areas of pain and breathing deeply into those areas, releasing the tension with each exhalation. Go back and check whether the tight or tired muscles have begun to relax. Count your blessings.

Always see yourself successfully dealing with the sticking points throughout the day—the times when you smoked in the past, or the triggers associated with your former smoking patterns.

Incorporate as much detail and positive thought as you can to make the visualization more real. See yourself as a non-smoker enjoying the many benefits of being free of smoking. See yourself rejoicing in the process of taking back control of your life. See yourself relieved that you don't have to worry about the health consequences of smoking. See yourself saying "no" to everything that has to do with nicotine and smoking.

101

LEARN BREATHING FROM
THE GURU OF GOOD HEALTH

Andrew Weil, M.D., author of *Health and Healing* and many other books, endorses medical practices that are far from the mainstream; however, if you read enough of the spa and health publications, you realize that the public has begun to embrace his ideas on healing.

Dr. Weil says that breathing is the most vital and mysterious function of the body. Many philosophers equate breathing with the spirit of life, which begins with the first breath and ends with the last.

Breathing is unique, as it is the only bodily function that can be completely voluntary or fully involuntary. Breathing also influences moods and emotions. Weil describes proper breathing as "a full, deep expansion of the lungs, with expiration at least as long as inspiration, and the rhythm of the breath is slow and quiet."

I suggest you try the following three breathing techniques to tone up your healing system and hasten your full recovery from nicotine addiction. You can do each one in a few minutes, and you will realize their full power if you practice them regularly.

Observe the Breath

102

Sit in a comfortable position with your eyes closed. Focus your attention on the breath without trying to influence it in any way. Follow the rhythm of the cycle and see if you can determine the points at which the cycle changes. This is a basic form of meditation, a relaxation method, and a way to harmonize the body, mind, and spirit.

Start with Exhalation

Breathing is continuous with no beginning or end, but we tend to think of one breath as starting with an inhalation and ending with an exhalation. Now reverse this perception and start with an exhalation. Focus on the breath without trying to change it. You have more control over exhalation because you can use the voluntary muscles between your ribs to squeeze air out of your lungs. These muscles are stronger than the ones used to inhale. When you move air out first, you will automatically take in more air. This deepened respiration brings more health-giving oxygen into the body.

Let Yourself Be Breathed

This exercise is best done while lying on your back; you may want to do it before going to sleep at night or upon waking up. Close your eyes, let your arms rest alongside your body, and focus attention on the breath without trying to influence it. Now imagine that with each inhalation, a higher power or your spiritual nature is blowing breath into you; and with each exhalation, withdrawing it. Let yourself feel the breath penetrating to every part of your body. Hold this perception through eight or ten breath cycles.

103

11

Exercise

TRAINING BODY AND MIND

Some coaches, particularly swimming coaches, estimate that as much as 70 percent of winning depends on the state of mind and only about 30 percent on the discipline of practice. All coaches would agree that one needs to train both the body and the mind to become a gold-medal winner.

Likewise, to win and hold your gold medal in the fight against nicotine, you now must train and discipline your body and mind. Like most athletes, you will probably find that the battle between positive and negative thoughts is most important as you head toward victory.

As I was working on this section of the book, Lance Armstrong won the 1999 Tour de France. Facing fearful odds from metastasized cancer, he regained his health and went on to win the most coveted bicycle race in the world. His story is extraordinary and is the kind of testimony to the human spirit we all can appreciate. You may think your battle against your adversary, nicotine, is less dramatic, but in fact you are being called upon to overcome obstacles that are as real to you as Armstrong's were to him.

THE SISYPHUS CONNECTION

The Greek myth of Sisyphus is similar to your efforts to obtain ultimate pleasure from smoking. Because he betrayed Zeus, Sisyphus's punishment was to push a large boulder up a mountain. Just before he got to the top, the rock rolled all the way back down the mountain. Sisyphus went back to the bottom of the mountain and pushed the boulder up again, but the same thing happened. The cycle never ended.

As a smoker, you tried to meet certain needs in your life by smoking cigarettes. You knew all the disadvantages, and they weighed heavy in your heart; nevertheless, you trudged upward to reach a high, solve your problems, and feel good about yourself. But notice that you never quite made it. Your body built up a tolerance to nicotine, and it managed to push you back down to diminish any pleasure from smoking. Nicotine's effect had decreased dramatically over time, even though your smoking pattern remained the same.

You were in the process of smoking away your time, money, and health, and eventually your self-respect. Yet until you learned a better way to deal with problems, you started the uphill trek again, loaded down by your cigarette addiction, in a vain search for a really satisfying high.

But you don't have to be like Sisyphus. Your life does not have to be controlled by fickle Greek gods or nicotine. You have the freedom to continue to choose natural highs that bring true and lasting satisfaction.

EXERCISE: A NATURAL HIGH

There is no question in my mind that exercising regularly and vigorously during the withdrawal period is the most significant component of any program to free yourself from tobacco. I have witnessed this phenomenon in my groups for many years.

Exercise offers you many of the things you have tried to gain from smoking. At the same time, exercise reduces withdrawal symptoms to a minimum.

The Stimulation of Nicotine versus Exercise

Inhaled nicotine reaches the brain in seven seconds, half the time it would take if it were injected into a vein. The nicotine causes the release of adrenaline, which produces a rise in blood pressure and heart rate. Glucose runs through the bloodstream and, along with oxygen, is rushed to the brain. The result is a subtle but definite high. This sensation is diminished in twenty or thirty minutes, and you soon find yourself with a feeling of depression you think can be relieved only by reaching for a cigarette.

Although nicotine triggers an initial rush of oxygen to the brain, smoking decreases the assimilation of oxygen in the blood by over 30 percent. Less total oxygen is available, which limits many smokers from enjoying serious athletics. Smokers get winded from even mild exercise such as walking on a simple incline. Since nicotine constricts the blood vessels, and the carbon monoxide in tobacco smoke ties up much of the hemoglobin in the red blood cells, there is an extra load on the heart, which must work hard to circulate the limited number of cells that can still carry oxygen. I often lead morning walks and have a reputation for going over the speed limit. I used to be astonished at how out of shape most people are. I urge you to start thinking of your body as a brand-new car you want to preserve.

MAKE EXERCISE A PART OF YOUR LIFE

The most important strategy in remaining free from smoking is to put an exercise component into your life. The major benefits of exercise are these:

- Exercise brings a true, natural, and sustained high.
- Exercise gives relief from tension, a benefit smokers falsely think they get from cigarettes.
- Exercise decreases neuromuscular tension and increases relaxation.
- Aerobic exercise slows and even reverses the aging process.
- The exercised heart pumps more blood with each stroke, so this efficiency saves 20 million superfluous heartbeats per year.

- Exercise offers a long-term reduction of both systolic and diastolic blood pressure.
- Exercise dilates blood vessels, allowing blood to circulate freely to the hands, feet, and surface areas of the body. (Most smokers complain of cold hands and feet.)
- Exercise can prevent the potential weight gain connected with breaking free of cigarettes.
- You can develop a healthy addiction to exercise, which will be manifested in many positive changes in addition to losing interest in cigarettes.

Choose the type of exercise that is best for you and stick with it for the rest of your life. Walking is the first and easiest choice for millions who have stopped smoking and is a great place to start.

UNDERSTAND THE FOUR ELEMENTS OF EXERCISE AND CHOOSE A PLAN

Physical fitness is most easily understood by examining its components. There is widespread agreement that the basic elements of exercise are (1) cardiorespiratory endurance, (2) flexibility through stretching, (3) muscular strength, and (4) muscular endurance.

Cardiorespiratory Endurance

Cardiorespiratory endurance is the ability to deliver oxygen and nutrients to tissues and to remove wastes over sustained periods of time. This is an elegant way to describe aerobic exercise.

In the 1950s, the rage for aerobic fitness resulted from studies conducted by Dr. Kenneth Cooper. It is well understood that aerobic exercise benefits the entire cardiovascular system and increases stamina. It also produces endorphins, which contribute to relaxation and mental alertness. Exercising your heart for as little as twenty minutes a day will contribute to a longer and better life. Long walks, runs, and swims are a good way to measure how your endurance is building up.

Flexibility Through Stretching

Stretching after every aerobic activity contributes to relaxation, increases muscular strength, improves circulation, and makes you more mentally alert. The goal of flexibility training is to move joints and use muscles through their full range of motion. Yoga is an excellent way to maintain flexibility. If you find yoga a bit intimidating, take a look at the list of essential body stretches at the end of this chapter.

Muscular Strength

The measure of a muscle's strength is its ability to exert force for a brief period of time. Upper-body strength can be measured by various weight-lifting exercises. Toning exercises focus on firming and toning your muscles.

Muscular Endurance

Muscular endurance is the ability of a muscle, or group of muscles, to sustain repeated contractions or to continue applying force against a fixed object.

Weight training uses resistance through movement to contract muscles. Working out on machines or free weights, at home or in a gym, with proper instruction will show positive results in a very short time. Push-ups and other resistance calisthenics also provide great benefit. The lean muscle mass built up through strength training will increase your basal metabolism rate and thus have a positive effect on the homeostasis of your body.

How often, how hard, and how long you exercise, as well as what kinds of exercise you choose, are all determined by your goals. Your present fitness level, your age, and your health are among the factors you need to think about when choosing an exercise.

Following are the amounts of activity necessary for the average, healthy person to maintain a minimum level of overall fitness. Popular choices for each of the four components of exercise are included.

111

Warm-Up

Before working out, do five to ten minutes of exercise such as walking, slow jogging, arm circles, or trunk rotations (like football players do). These are low-intensity movements that prepare you for the movements you will be doing in the aerobic section.

Cardiorespiratory Endurance

Plan at least three 20-minute bouts a week of continuous aerobic exercise. This could include brisk walking, jogging, swimming, cycling, jumping rope, rowing, cross-country skiing, and vigorous games like racquetball and handball.

Flexibility

Conclude all aerobic or muscular-endurance activities with a ten- to twelve-minute stretching regime, performed slowly without a bouncing motion.

Muscular Strength

Every week, do a minimum of two 20-minute sessions that include exercises for all the major muscle groups. Lifting weights is the most effective way to increase strength, and you can do it while watching TV or participating in some other passive activity.

Muscular Endurance

Do at least three 30-minute sessions a week that include exercises such as old-fashioned calisthenics, push-ups, sit-ups, pull-ups, and weight training for all the major muscle groups.

Cooldown

After any muscular or aerobic session, allow your body to cool down with a minimum of five to ten minutes of slow walking, or another low-level exercise, combined with stretching.

To summarize:

1. Warm-up: 5 to 10 minutes, daily
2. Aerobics: 30 minutes, three times a week
3. Stretching: 10 to 12 minutes, daily
4. Muscular strength: 20 minutes, two times a week
5. Muscular endurance: 30 minutes, three times a week
6. Cooldown: 5 to 10 minutes, daily

WALKING

Let me emphasize once again that the most useful exercise is walking. Think of walking as a form of meditation, relaxation, and transportation. When you know that you can walk comfortably for at least half an hour, at a pace of fifteen minutes per mile, you can begin to plan your day so that walking is fun and rewarding.

STARTING OFF
ON THE RIGHT FOOT

Whenever starting a new exercise program, you'll want to ease into it slowly. The old saying "no pain, no gain" may be catchy, but it's not sound advice. A good way to pace yourself at the beginning is to make sure you're able to talk comfortably during your walk. As you progress, you can gradually push yourself harder. Take your time. Your body is not going to change overnight, particularly if you've been smoking for a long time. Whatever your level of activity, use common sense.

AN EASY, DOABLE
STRETCHING ROUTINE

One common mistake made by those who exercise is not stretching. To prevent soreness and possible injury, be sure to stretch your muscles every day. Remember to stretch gently, hold for at least ten seconds, then stretch a little farther and hold for another ten to twenty seconds.

Calves

Facing a wall, place one foot flat on the ground two to three feet from the wall. Place the heel of the other foot near enough to the wall to prop your foot against it at a 45- to 60-degree angle. Push against the wall with your knee straight for ten seconds, then with your knee bent for ten seconds. Repeat with your other leg.

Quadriceps (Front of Thigh)

Stand near a sturdy table, or something else that is waist-high and can be grasped for support. Place one hand on the table and reach behind with the other one, lifting the foot on the same side. Grasp your ankle and pull gently until you feel the muscle stretch. Hold for twenty seconds. Turn around and repeat on the other side.

Hamstrings

Stand with your feet as far apart as possible. Reach for the toes on one foot, then the other. Stay down for a full minute if possible. This is also good for stretching your lower back.

Hip Flexors

Stand with one foot two feet behind the other. Point both feet forward. Keeping the back leg straight, bend the front leg at the knee until you feel the pull at the top of your back leg. Repeat with the other leg.

Lower Back

Lie down, wrap your arms around your shins, and pull your knees to your chest.

Upper Body

Reach for the sky and arch your back.

This would be a good time to incorporate exercises such as leg lifts, jumping jacks, or sit-ups into your routine.

THE BODY MACHINE:
A MARVELOUS "CHIP"

115

Your body is an incredible vehicle, designed with precision to serve you well for many years—within a certain lifestyle and environmental framework. Up to the early 1900s, good health occurred naturally: people ate a variety of healthful foods and exercised their bodies by working and walking. Our present-day environmental conditions are drastically different.

The quality of life has improved in many ways over the past century. Thanks to the miracles of modern science, we are able to fulfill our needs faster and more easily than ever before. Yet ironically, most of our health problems today (including obesity, hypertension, and heart disease) are a direct result of our easier lifestyle. Convenience is a good thing, but we've simply got too much of a good thing. All that convenience we enjoy must be balanced with exercise.

There are, of course, lots of excuses to avoid exercise: "I might hurt myself"; "I can't afford to join a club or go to a spa"; or the most commonly used excuse, "I just don't have the time." Now that you are free of smoking, you'll have plenty of healthy years in which to continue to save your life.

When is the best time to exercise? This is a frequent question asked by those going through nicotine withdrawal, and there is a very good answer. The best time to exercise is when you least want to. Exercise will change your mood immediately, and you will congratulate yourself for making the effort.

116

EXERCISE RESOURCES

Do a little research:

- Find a health club close to your home or office. If you like what the club offers, and you can afford it, sign up for a three-month trial program.
- Study the newspaper section that lists group exercise activities such as walking clubs, hiking clubs, bicycling groups, volleyball, and tennis.
- Look into water aerobics or water walking; these activities are extremely popular.
- Convince your partner or a friend that exercise is going to keep you off cigarettes forever, and plan to exercise together.
- Park your car a good distance away and walk to work or to go shopping.
- If you have a hard time getting started, get a personal trainer.

A friend gave me a wonderful pin that has the word *attitude* spelled out in gold. It is attached on a pivot pin, so I often have to adjust it. Now it is time to adjust your attitude toward exercise. The fact that you smoked for so long probably made you avoid participating in a meaningful exercise program. You now have the time to investigate and plan a regimen that will keep you moving and be enjoyable. You have the courage to give up cigarettes. Take the next small step and give your body the chance to reflect your mind's glory. Go for it!

12

Avoiding
Weight Gain

SMOKING CESSATION
AND WEIGHT GAIN

You don't have to gain weight after breaking free of cigarettes. The authors of the *Breathe Free Plan to Stop Smoking* state that among people who stop smoking, one-third loses weight, one-third stays the same, and one-third gains weight. It is this last third who feel additional stress during the process of quitting smoking.

You must understand that if you are already overweight, stopping smoking has dramatically increased your life expectancy and may have given you the self-confidence to address weight loss. I can't tell you to stop worrying, but I do believe that with the right attitude you can avoid any significant weight gain. If you put on a few extra pounds, you can choose healthy ways to return to normal.

INCREASING METABOLISM

The basal metabolic rate (BMR) is a number that indicates how efficiently the body burns calories. With a high BMR, you will burn more fat and have an easier time losing weight and maintaining your ideal body weight.

The conventional wisdom is that smoking cigarettes increases your metabolism and that when you stop smoking you will have to make up the difference in some way, or else you'll gain weight. Fear of weight gain is the reason most often given for refusing to take the first step in becoming smoke-free, and is often the reason people relapse and return to smoking.

For many years, it has been my challenge to find out the exact percentage by which a smoker's metabolism is increased. After an intensive Internet search, I found a study listed by the Health, Mind & Body Resource Center that concluded that "smoking increases the BMR by 10 percent."

There are two options that should help prevent weight gain after stopping smoking: You can increase your BMR by increasing the number of calories you burn, which you can do by exercising 10 percent more than you do now; or you can decrease the calories you consume by 10 percent.

There is, however, a trap in this theory. Two out of three people who go on a diet will regain the weight in one year or less, and 97 percent will regain the weight in five years. To make matters worse, when dieters go back to their old way of eating, they often end up weighing more than they did before they began dieting. They have violated the most important rule in creating and maintaining a healthy, rapid metabolism—lose fat, not lean muscle mass.

The simple solution to avoiding weight gain is to get into a workout program that tones your muscles and increases their mass. All it takes to add 10 pounds of muscle is a regular weight-training program involving only thirty minutes, three times a week, for about six months. The wonderful thing about increasing metabolism through building more muscle is that you don't have to think about the number of calories you take in. Refer to chapter 11 for specific exercises you can do, or consult with a personal trainer who can give you a plan suited to your body type and needs.

A HIGH-ALKALINE DIET
FOR HEALTH AND WEIGHT STABILITY

If you are concerned about weight gain, you probably know a good deal about how difficult it is to lose weight without feeling hungry and deprived. High-protein diets seem to take care of that problem, but you should pay particular attention to the side effects of such plans. The Mediterranean diet is the most sensible plan to incorporate into your new lifestyle. I am particularly impressed by the book *Low-Fat Lies: High-Fat Frauds and the Healthiest Diet in the World,* in which Kevin Vigilante and Mary Flynn take the confusion out of the extremely diverse rules that come from the various so-called experts on nutrition and weight loss. Vigilante and Flynn have developed their own food pyramid, based on the Mediterranean diet, which is sensible and understandable and offers a middle ground between low-fat, high-fiber diets and super-high-fat, high-protein weight-loss programs.

Frequent meals keep the metabolism energized. While the usual dieter will often skip meals, it is essential that you never miss breakfast.

In a study conducted by the UCLA Medical Center on 10,000 people who lived beyond their life expectancy, seven rules of good health were listed. Not smoking was, of course, at the top of the list, but one thing these people all had in common was that they ate breakfast.

When you don't eat breakfast, a temporary fasting state sends a signal to your body that food is in short supply. As a result, the stress hormones (including cortisone) increase and the body begins shutting down and shedding its lean muscle tissue. Decreasing this metabolically active tissue will decrease the body's need for food. When you next take in food, the sensitized pancreas will sharply increase blood insulin levels, which is the body's signal to make fat. Eating small meals frequently (grazing) will decrease cholesterol by 15 percent, decrease insulin by 28 percent, and help prevent carbohydrates and proteins from being converted to fat.

13

How Cigarettes Affect the Body and Mind

WHAT SMOKING DOES TO YOUR BODY

There is now a vast body of evidence—including hundreds of epidemiological, experimental, pathological, and clinical studies—that demonstrate how smoking increases the smoker's risk of death and illness from a wide variety of diseases.

In July 1999, the first class-action suit against the tobacco companies was won in Florida. This has had a wide influence on the public's awareness of the harmful effects of cigarettes. Many nicotine-addicted invalids will collect great sums of money because their health is irreversibly impaired. Yet to so many others who are not yet sick, smoking is a game of roulette: each cigarette they smoke is like placing a bet. The "prize" is a heart attack, lung cancer, or some other disease. If your "number" comes up, you've had it, but if you are "lucky" and your number never comes up, you can avoid the hazardous consequences of smoking altogether and live to a ripe old age, totally unaffected by your smoking habit.

This is not only a serious misconception, but an outright lie. Every cigarette you smoke harms your body. True, some smokers have lived into their seventies and eighties without stopping. But don't kid yourself that you'll be one of them. They almost certainly suffered substantial physical impairment while they were alive as the result of their smoking. Young smokers may have already noted some problems but choose to ignore these symptoms, using these older smokers to rationalize that smoking is okay. If these older smokers had not smoked, they probably would have lived even longer.

Inside a Smoker's Body

Let's take a look at what happens inside your body each time you light up. Think about how quickly tobacco smoke can produce harmful effects.

Eyes, Nose, Throat

Within a few seconds of your first puff, irritating gases (form-aldehyde, ammonia, hydrogen sulfide, and others) begin to work on sensitive membranes of your eyes, nose, and throat. Your eyes water, your nose runs, and your throat is irritated. If you continue smoking, these irritating gases will contribute to your smoker's cough.

Continued smoking produces abnormal thickening in the membranes lining your throat, accompanied by cellular changes that resemble those that occur in throat cancer.

Lungs

Continued exposure can completely paralyze the lungs' natural cleansing process.

- Your respiratory rate increases, forcing your lungs to work harder.
- Irritating gases produce chemical injury to the tissues of your lungs. This speeds up the production of mucus and leads to an increased tendency to cough up sputum.
- Excess mucus serves as a breeding ground for a variety of bacteria and viruses. You become more susceptible to colds, flu, bronchitis, and other respiratory infections. And if you do come down with an infection, your body is less able to fight it, because smoking impairs the ability of the white blood cells to fight invading organisms.
- The lining of your bronchi begins to thicken, predisposing you to cancer. Most lung cancers arise in the bronchial lining.
- Smoke weakens the free-roving scavenger cells that remove foreign particles from the air sacs of the lungs. Continued smoke exposure adversely affects elastin (the enzyme that keeps your lungs flexible), predisposing you to emphysema.
- Many of the compounds you inhale are deposited as a layer of sticky tar on the lining of your throat and bronchi and in the delicate air sacs of your lungs. A pack-a-day smoker pours about a pint—16 ounces— of tar into his or her lungs each year. This tar is rich in cancer-producing chemicals.

125

Heart

From the moment smoke reaches your lungs, your heart is forced to work harder. It beats an extra 10 to 25 times per minute, or as many as 36,000 additional times per day.

Because of the irritating effect of nicotine and other components of tobacco smoke, your heartbeat is more likely to be irregular. A recent Surgeon General's report estimated that each year about 170,000 heart attacks are caused by smoking. Another unofficial statistic in the literature is that half of smokers' first heart attacks are fatal. In other words, if you are smoking and you have a heart attack, you have only a fifty-fifty chance of survival. Between 75 and 80 percent of survivors stop smoking after their first heart attack.

Blood Vessels

Your blood pressure increases by 10 to 15 percent every time you light up, putting additional stress on your heart and blood vessels and increasing your risk of heart attack and stroke. Smoking increases your risk of Berger's disease, which cuts off virtually all the circulation in your extremities. Severe cases require amputation. About eight years ago, a surgeon from Texas came to one of my sessions to learn how to stop smoking. He had performed several amputations that were directly related to smoking.

Skin

Smoking constricts the blood vessels in your skin, decreasing the delivery of life-giving oxygen to the largest organ in your body. This, combined with the damaging rays of the sun, causes premature wrinkling in smokers. I have shown a fairly graphic film in my workshops that depicts the horribly wrinkled skin of women smokers in their fifties. And I have testimonies saying that seeing this film was a positive motivator to break free of smoking.

If vanity were more compelling a motivator, more smokers would break free, because they are at high risk for a medical syndrome commonly called "smoker's face." This is characterized by deep lines around the corners of the mouth and eyes, a gauntness of facial features, and a grayish appearance of the skin. In one study, 46 percent of long-term smokers were found to have smoker's face.

Blood

Carbon monoxide—the colorless, odorless, deadly gas present in automobile exhaust—is present in cigarette smoke in more than 600 times the concentration considered safe in industrial plants. A smoker's blood typically contains four to fifteen times as much carbon monoxide as that of a nonsmoker. This carbon monoxide stays in the bloodstream for up to six hours after you stop smoking. You decrease your likelihood of sudden death by 50 percent within a few hours of ceasing smoking.

When you breathe in cigarette smoke, the carbon monoxide passes immediately into your blood, binding to the oxygen receptor sites and expelling the oxygen molecules from your red blood cells. This means that less oxygen reaches your brain and other vital organs. Because of this added carbon monoxide load, a smoker's red blood cells are also less effective in removing carbon dioxide in the gas-exchange system that occurs in the lungs.

Longtime smokers have abnormally high levels of red blood cells—a condition called polycythemia. In addition,

127

smoking makes your blood clot more easily. Both of these factors markedly increase your risk of heart attack or stroke.

Male Reproductive System

Two studies conducted at the New England Male Reproductive Health Center, at Boston University Medical School, found a possible link between smoking and erectile problems. In the first study, the researchers found that among a population of 1,101 men with erectile problems, 78 percent were smokers. The researchers concluded that decreased potency might result from the effect of smoking on the blood vessels leading to the male reproductive organs.

In addition to diminishing potency, smoking adversely affects the fertility of male smokers by decreasing sperm count and sperm mobility as well as altering the shape of sperm.

Female Reproductive System

Women who smoke heavily show a 43 percent decline in fertility and are three times more likely than nonsmokers to be infertile.

WHY SMOKING
MAKES YOU LESS FIT

Although a smoker's blood carries less oxygen, the nicotine in tobacco smoke increases the heart rate, requiring more oxygen. This is why smokers become short of breath more easily than nonsmokers. In *The Smoker's Book of Health,* Tom Ferguson points out that "subjects with a smoking history show a consistent impairment in performance at all stages of training when compared to subjects who have never smoked." The high concentration of carbon monoxide also reduces the level of oxygen that is carried to the brain. This can produce lethargy, confusion, and difficulty in thinking clearly.

SMOKING IMPAIRS TASTE AND SMELL

Continued smoking will result in a loss of a smoker's ability to taste and smell. This occurs so gradually that it may go unnoticed, but the end result is the decreased sensitivity of these two very important sense perceptions. These senses tend to return after smoking cessation, but seldom to maximum capacity.

129

SMOKERS DIE YOUNGER

No one disputes the fact that smokers die younger. In my workshops, I show a film titled "The Feminine Mistake," which features a tragic segment about a middle-aged woman dying of lung cancer. Emaciated and bald, she says, "I knew that smoking would shorten my life—but on the other end, not this end. I'm only forty-five." The impact of that kind of rationalization is overwhelming. I believe that this film has influenced many smokers to think about their mortality.

Below is a general summary of how many years of life smokers give up in exchange for smoking:

- light smokers give up 4.6 years
- moderate smokers give up 5.5 years
- heavy smokers give up 6.2 years
- very heavy smokers give up 8.3 years

LUNG AND OTHER CANCERS

Cancer is one of the most feared words in the English language. It is simply the word used to describe the abnormal growth of cells that may result in the destruction of healthy tissues. Persons exposed to certain environmental carcinogens are at increased risk for some cancers. Smokers who inhale tobacco smoke have a substantially increased risk for lung cancer. They are also at higher risk for cancers of the larynx, mouth, esophagus, bladder, kidney, and pancreas.

The National Institutes of Health did an analysis of how nicotine attacks the body and determined percentage of deaths from various diseases attributable to smoking.

SMOKERS HAVE MORE ILLNESSES

In addition to dying younger, smokers have increased rates of both acute and chronic illnesses. The U.S. Public Health Service has estimated that cigarettes are responsible for:

- 81 million missed days of work per year
- 145 million days spent ill in bed every year
- 11 million additional cases of chronic illnesses per year

130

PERCENTAGE OF DEATHS FROM DISEASES ATTRIBUTABLE TO SMOKING	
Lung cancer	85–90 percent
Bronchitis and emphysema	85 percent
Mouth cancer	70 percent
Throat cancer	50 percent
Bladder cancer	30–50 percent
Esophagus cancer	20–40 percent
Pancreas cancer	35 percent
Arteriosclerosis	33 percent
Heart disease	30 percent
Kidney disease	15–25 percent

131

- 280,000 additional cases of heart disease
- 1 million additional cases of chronic bronchitis and emphysema
- 1.8 million additional cases of chronic sinus problems
- 1 million additional cases of peptic ulcer

EFFECTS OF TOBACCO SMOKE
ON NONSMOKERS

Nonsmokers exposed to smoke-filled rooms show levels of carbon monoxide in their blood equivalent to those of light smokers. Among adults exposed to tobacco smoke, the most common symptoms are eye irritation, headache, nasal irritation, and coughing. Exposure to smoke can also trigger or aggravate allergic symptoms. Respiratory illness is more common in children exposed to tobacco smoke. And there is now considerable evidence to suggest that secondhand exposure to smoke increases the risk of both heart attacks and lung cancer.

14

Avoiding Relapse

ONE PUFF IS TOO MANY

The above is a paraphrase of the Alcoholics Anonymous edict to
not have even one more drink. This message is just as powerful
for smokers.

I hope chapter 4 made it clear that you are closely bound
to nicotine. To stay free, you need to accept how vulnerable you
are to being dragged back into the cigarette trap. Throughout
your smoking life, you denied the fact that cigarettes were the
driving force in your life—that you were addicted. Every unsuc-
cessful attempt you made to stop smoking proved this truth. You
must accept your vulnerable condition now and make the right
choice not to flirt with danger. If you choose to experiment with
a few cigarettes after you have been free for an extended time,

you will probably continue to smoke until your health is severely impaired. The truth is that for you, one puff is too many and ten thousand is not enough.

Why is one puff too many? First, look at your smoking habit for what it was: a way of life, not an occasional pastime. If you choose to take a puff after you have broken free, you will not stop there, because that puff is actually a choice to live a certain way. You once smoked all day, every day. You won't be able to stop now after one puff, as I'm sure you're aware.

You also need to realize that even though you tried, you would never have been able to cut down on your cigarette consumption, for one simple reason: You probably were smoking your minimum before you made the choice to stop. If cutting down was the path to freedom, it would have worked.

But in truth, cutting down usually results in going back to or exceeding your former rate of consumption. You don't really want just a puff. Nor do you want just a cigarette. You are someone who wants to smoke a lot of cigarettes.

If you should take that one puff, you would set in motion the plan for the rest of your life. If you smoke only one pack a day and live ten more years, you will smoke 73,000 cigarettes. Think of those cigarettes pushing through your front door, relentlessly filling up your house. If you say, "I only want one puff now, and then I won't smoke any more," you are lying to yourself and inviting the flood of cigarettes.

Facing reality can be tough. It's not usually what you want it to be. The reality of your situation is that you don't want just a puff; you want to *smoke*. To remain free of your addiction, you need to be honest about who you are and what your problem

134

is. You are a smoker. The only choices reality gives you are to choose total freedom from smoking and gain the benefits thereof, or to take a puff and smoke until you die.

In the next few days, you will have to concentrate on all the skills you need to avoid relapse. The battle from now on is in your mind and in your imagination.

I don't like to think about the possibility of your going back to smoking. Since you have gotten this far into the book, I must assume you have had success in breaking free of cigarettes. So why would you ever go back? Think of the many benefits you have achieved in a short time: your lung capacity has increased by at least 15 percent, your cough has disappeared, you no longer fear going to the doctor, you are now in control of your life. With all this going for you, how could you possibly think of going back to the drug that once possessed you?

135

DEALING WITH A SMOKING PARTNER

As I have told my graduates for many years, the biggest challenge for someone trying to remain smoke free is living with a smoking partner. If this is your situation, you can use all of your negotiation powers to set boundaries as to where and when your partner can smoke. Remember the significance of the Serenity Prayer (see page 18) and emphasize to your partner how you have changed. If your partner is willing to help you develop your personal mission statement (see page 136), you can probably work out long- and short-term strategies to deal with the difference in your lifestyles.

YOUR PERSONAL MISSION STATEMENT

Every company, and many volunteer organizations, write mission statements that proclaim where they are and where they're going. Take a minute to write a statement of your personal mission as it pertains to your body, mind, and spirit. This is a difficult chore, but with a positive image of the future and the present, along with passion and enthusiasm, the course is more easily charted. There is no right or wrong. Just write it down and see if returning to the enslavement of nicotine fits into the picture. When you have a clearer image of where you are and where you want to be, you will be able to handle your feelings in a more positive way.

DEALING WITH FEELINGS

Most smokers admit they used cigarettes to deal with or muffle such feelings as boredom, frustration, anger, or nervousness. If you try to remove the cigarettes from your life without figuring out some other coping skills to deal with tough feelings, you might be setting yourself up for relapse.

Psychologists identify five major categories of feelings:

1. Mad
2. Sad
3. Glad
4. Afraid
5. Ashamed

Of course, there are many variations within each of these categories, and sometimes we call one feeling by another name.

I mentioned these feelings to one of my groups, and one participant said that nothing in the list adequately described the feeling of irritation one has in the initial stages of breaking free. No one disagreed.

Identify Your Feelings

You may have discovered when you composed your mission statement that it is often difficult to identify your feelings. Many of us are not aware of the range of our feelings.

Review your reasons for breaking free of cigarettes listed on page 37. Ask yourself if you feel satisfied that you are achieving these goals. Are your reasons to be free tied into your mission statement? As soon as you become aware of your feelings, and what "triggers" them, you will be able to cope with them without cigarettes.

Taking responsibility or "ownership" of your feelings is critically important in learning to cope. Sharing these feelings with someone you trust is helpful, as this person can help you go through the process of sorting them out. Discussing your most painful emotions (such as anger, fear, and loneliness) and permitting yourself to go through the pain of losing cigarettes is time well spent.

You may need help in dealing with the feelings that come up after you have broken free of cigarettes. Chapter 5 features a long list of possible support groups. If you're not a "groupie," take a chance on one meeting, just to see what it feels like. One recent graduate of my program found a virtual support group on the Internet.

137

A support system is an important means of getting help in processing your feelings and will improve the odds of a successful recovery. Often, expressing or owning your negative feelings about certain people in your life will help you to let go of these feelings. If this should fail to work, and you find yourself harboring resentment, you can ask your friends to confront you if they sense that you are feeling resentful and not dealing with it.

The members of an effective group support system will help you by:

- Listening to you without trying to "fix" you
- Asking you to define your feelings more precisely
- Confronting you with specific facts, but without passing judgment
- Encouraging you to recognize how far you have come and to emphasize the positive

Because of their personal involvement with you, family and some friends may be less able to help you than a support group or others going through the process of breaking free of cigarettes.

BE PATIENT: YOU'VE COME A LONG WAY

You have spent years developing your coping skills, most of which have involved smoking. New coping skills aren't developed easily. Continue to take a "one day at a time" attitude. When you find yourself in a difficult or tense situation, stop to identify, own, and let go of your feelings. This will help you deal effectively with your emotions, rather than just react to them.

DRINKING AND INCREASED STRESS

Alcohol and stress are the two major factors in smoking relapse, and are directly tied into dealing or not dealing with negative feelings.

Be aware of and celebrate your positive progress. Give yourself a hug and a pat on the back several times a day, which is also a great way to stretch your tense arms and shoulders. When you experience a feeling in the "glad" category, stop and rejoice. Humor, joy, and happy feelings are similar to the endorphins that counteract stress and bring us natural highs. The more we can build such natural means of coping, the less susceptible we will be to artificial coping methods such as nicotine, alcohol, or the many toxic pharmaceuticals prescribed today to help people deal with feelings.

139

THE TWELVE STEPS

Alcoholics Anonymous has been one of the most successful programs to help people overcome their addiction to alcohol. The principles AA teaches are worth looking into for tobacco and nicotine addiction. There is, however, a difference in the consequences of these addictions, which influences how people view them: alcohol addiction ruins your life; addiction to nicotine ruins your health. Many AA meetings are smoke-free, and you can attend them as part of your support plan. Both AA and Nicotine Anonymous follow the twelve steps and offer telephone hot lines.

Following are the twelve steps of AA. They carry a powerful message to millions of people:

1. We admitted we were powerless over alcohol—that our lives had become unmanageable.
2. Came to believe that a Power greater than ourselves could restore us to sanity.
3. Made a decision to turn our will and our lives over to the care of God as we understood Him.
4. Made a searching and fearless moral inventory of ourselves.
5. Admitted to God, to ourselves and to another human being the exact nature of our wrongs.
6. Were entirely ready to have God remove all these defects of character.

7. Humbly asked Him to remove our shortcomings.
8. Made a list of all persons we had harmed, and became willing to make amends to them all.
9. Made direct amends to such people wherever possible, except when to do so would injure them or others.
10. Continued to take personal inventory and when we were wrong promptly admitted it.
11. Sought through prayer and meditation to improve our conscious contact with God, as we understood Him, praying only for knowledge of His will for us and the power to carry that out.
12. Having had a spiritual awakening as the result of these steps, we tried to carry this message to alcoholics, and to practice these principles in all our affairs.

RECOMMENDED READING

Baer, Andrea. *Quit Smoking for Good: A Supportive Program for Permanent Smoking Cessation.* Freedom, Calif.: The Crossing Press, 1998. Reviews the steps followed personally by the author.

Casey, Karen. *If Only I Could Quit: Becoming a Nonsmoker.* Center City, Minn.: Hazelden Information and Education Services, 1987. Recounts stories of several people who struggled with cigarette addiction. Offers ninety days of meditations to stay on course.

Csikszentmihalyi, Mihaly. *Flow: The Psychology of Optimal Experience.* New York: HarperPerennial, 1991. Summarizes for the general audience decades of research on the positive aspects of human experience: joy, creativity, and the process of total involvement that the author calls "flow."

Delaney, Sue F. *Women Smokers Can Quit: A Different Approach.* Evanston, Ill.: Women's Health Care Press, 1989. Explains women's issues in regard to smoking cessation and offers positive reinforcement.

Ferguson, Tom. *The Smoker's Book of Health: How to Keep Yourself Healthier and Reduce Your Smoking Risks.* New York: Ballantine Books, 1988. Details the negative effects of smoking.

Holmes, Peter and Peggy Holmes. *Out of the Ashes: Help for People Who Have Quit Smoking.* Minneapolis, Minn.: Fairview Press, 1992. Meditations based on the personal struggles of many individuals who have been able to stop smoking.

U.S. Department of Health and Human Services, Public Health Service. *Smoking Cessation, Clinical Practice Guideline #18.* AHCPR Publication No. 9800692, April 1996. This guideline contains strategies and recommendations to assist smoking cessation specialists.

Rustin, Terry A. *Quit and Stay Quit: A Personal Program to Stop Smoking.* Center City, Minn.: Hazelden Information and Education Services, 1991. Workbook by twelve-step specialist for promoting day-to-day recovery from nicotine dependence.

Schachter, Stanley, ed., and Neil E. Grunberg. *A Distinctive Approach to Psychological Research: The Influence of Stanley Schachter.* Hillsdale, N.J.: Lawrence Erlbaum Assoc., 1987. Includes studies on the effects of nicotine on the human brain.

Vigilante, Kevin, and Mary Flynn. *Low-Fat Lies: High-Fat Frauds and the Healthiest Diet in the World.* New York: Regnery Publishing, May 1999. Overview of high-fat diet frauds and the "healthiest diet in the world"—the Mediterranean diet.

INDEX